REMOTE VIEWING

UFOS AND THE VISITORS

WHERE DO THEY COME FROM?

WHAT ARE THEY?

WHO ARE THEY?

WHY ARE THEY HERE?

TUNDE ATUNRASE

REMOTE VIEWING UFOS AND THE VISITORS, *WHERE DO THEY COME FROM? WHAT ARE THEY? WHO ARE THEY? WHY ARE THEY HERE?* - **Tunde Atunrase**

First Edition 2015

10 9 8 7 6 5 4 3 2 1

ISBN-13: 978-1512115444

ISBN-10: 1512115444

Cover Design by John Moore Noir33.com

Photo by Nick Lawrence

*"Remote Viewing (RV) is the ability to perceive and communicate accurate information about places, people, concepts or events, under an appropriately **'blind'** protocol, without regard to distance, space or time."*

ACKNOWLEDGEMENTS

This has probably been the hardest thing I've ever done and it was never my intention to write a book like this. What started out as a simple private quest for answers to an enigma, somehow took on a life of its own. I was privy to so much amazing remote viewing information it felt almost *criminal* not to reveal some of that information with other like-minded souls who share the same thirst for answers as I do.

I would also like to add, this book could not have been possible without the help and knowledge of one person who guided me towards the services of Joe McMoneagle all those years ago.
Palyne 'PJ' Gaenir, this is for you and all your selfless hard work and dedication to Project TKR and remote viewing in general - *Thank You.*

Joe McMoneagle - Remote Viewer #001
You are truly something else. Thank you for your time and words of wisdom. It's been an absolute honour working with you. I hope the world gets to see feedback on some of the incredible things you came up with. None of this would be possible without your contribution and I can't say thank you enough.

Nancy 'Scooter' McMoneagle
What can I say? Thank you for all your help and advice over the years. Virgos Rock ☺

Paul H. Smith Ph.D
Thank you for your words of wisdom prior to publishing this work and your expert advice. I am eternally grateful and honoured that you took the time and effort to write the foreword for this book.

I would also like to thank the following who have been there from the very beginning of this crazy journey. Jean Thornton, Pru Calabrese, Jon Knowles, Daz Smith, Elizabeth Ruse, Kay Lakka, Jade, Don Williams, Don Walker, Larry Digges, Marv Darley, Mike Faber, Bill Moulton, Damien Vanier, Evelyn Niedbalec, Glyn Carr, John Cook, Roma Zanders, Sulo Nair, Julie Choi, Rumana Zahn, Rick and Sandra Hilleard, Arlene Rose Dockery, Charlene Dockery, Fortune Fairchild, Michelle Reed, John Vivanco, Laura Fallon, BEI and Angela T Smith Ph.D.

Special thanks to John Burroughs, Jim Penniston, Michael Hessman, Albert S Rosales, Nick Lawrence (photo), Dr Joaquim Fernandez , Fina D' Armada, Dr Ardy Sixkiller Clark, Travis Walton, Lance W. Beem, Debra L. Katz and Richard D Hall.

Those who have influenced and inspired me over the years deserve a mention, Jean Millay Ph.D, Timothy Good, Lyn Buchanan, Paul H Smith Ph.D, Dick Allgire, Hitomi Akamatsu, Stephan Schwartz, Ed May Ph.D, David Morehouse Ph.D, Jacques Vallee, Carl Sagan, Russell Targ, Ingo Swann, Dolores Cannon and of course once again – Joe McMoneagle.

"Qui Vivra Verra"

He who lives to *see*, will *know*

TABLE OF CONTENTS

DEDICATIONS

For Mum,

Isabelle & Mya

FOREWORD

By

Paul H. Smith, Ph.D. (Major, US Army, ret.)

Near the end of 1995, when the CIA publicly acknowledged the existence of a government-sponsored program that trained and used psychic spies to gather intelligence about America's foreign opponents, the revelation immediately caught the attention of people around the world. The fact that the news coincided with the emergence of the World Wide Web allowed this attention to spread widely, giving people from every corner of the globe a forum where they could exchange views and new experiences as they first researched, and then learned to perform this newly-available extrasensory skill.

Like thousands of others, Tunde Atunrase joined in the digital conversation almost from the very beginning. He was a regular poster on several of the most active online groups, and he and I interacted frequently. We often disagreed, sometimes vehemently, but it was never personal, and I think we both recognized that such disagreements are an inevitable part of the emergence of a frontier field in the understanding of the human mind. I think we both learned a lot from each other. At least I know I did.

Unlike most of the keyboard warriors of those early days of excitement about remote viewing, he actually did more than just talk about it. To be fair, many of the others did take steps to learn how to use remote viewing to one degree or another, as did Tunde. But he also reached out to those more skilled and experienced than he (most notably legendary remote viewer Joe McMoneagle), and at his own expense engaged their abilities to help him investigate mysteries and conundrums that had long puzzled him.

One of the things I appreciate about Tunde's approach is how faithful he was (and is) to the need for rigorous protocols in conducting his projects. He knows that to be able to trust the results, the controls have to be impeccable.

I am also encouraged that Tunde is willing to follow where the data leads – even if it isn't in the direction he was first inclined to go. Many people are so invested in the UFO phenomenon that they are unwilling to accept anything but an extraterrestrial explanation for what is observed. Tunde admits surprise, but not dismay when some remote viewing data shows that long-cherished UFO events are not what he believed them to be.

There are things here that (preserving our common history together) I might argue with. But regardless of that, this is a worthwhile book. Like Tunde, I am fully convinced that there is intelligent life elsewhere in the universe besides here on Earth. And I happily accuse the current scientific skeptics of forming common cause with the medieval clerics in dogmatically asserting that the only intelligent life is here. But also like Tunde, I am wary of many of the claims I hear about unexplained aerial phenomena and extraterrestrial visitation. In my opinion, up to ninety percent of what is said in the UFO community is bunk.

Which is why I find Tunde's book refreshing. There is much that is speculative, but for the most part he delineates between fact and speculation, and when he uses remote viewing data as a starting point, he only considers that which was done under clean protocols. (This is in contrast to others who glibly accept *any* data that claims to be gotten from remote viewing, no matter how sloppy it is.) Of course, we all must be cautious of remote viewing even when done impeccably. Viewers can, after all, sometimes inadvertently inject their own analysis and preconceptions into the process, once they become aware through their viewing what the substance of the targeted event actually is. Tunde seems appropriately cautious in how he accepts and builds upon the thought-provoking remote viewing results that provide the foundation for this book.

Finally, I admire the lengths and considerable expense gone to in developing the content of this book. Without the author's determination and effort, we would not have these remote viewing gems from the legendary Joe McMoneagle. Even if that were the book's only virtue (which it is not), this would still be a valuable work of interest to generations to come.

Paul H. Smith, Ph.D. (Major, US Army, ret.)

March 26, 2015

Cedar City, Utah

Former Project Star Gate Operational Remote Viewer and best-selling author of *Reading the Enemy's Mind: Inside Star Gate: America's Psychic Espionage Program.*

Introduction

On Remote Viewing, and Joseph McMoneagle

I n the modern world, where proper skepticism is a good thing, and especially on the internet, where truth is even more arbitrary than usual, there is a niche-of-niche field around a practice called *Remote Viewing (RV)*. In a 'legitimacy' sense, it's populated only by people who explore or employ the (evolving, as they do) science-derived protocol for psi work, which spawned the label RV. But in a 'real-world' sense, it's populated by such an immense amount of marketing, fraud, commercialism, cultism, mis- and dis-information and even sheer lunacy that it's amazing anybody with a critical mind ever gets past all that to the real thing.

Sometimes people do. And what they find there is so mind-blowing that it can cause cognitive dissonance and great distress even to observers, let alone to people directly involved. Real viewing isn't a trick or even an intuitive mentalist skill. Once you see it done well under even the "firmest" protocol (precog-tasked, double-blind, hard-feedback), and repeatedly no less, you begin to realize it's something for which our culture has no explanation.

More importantly, it is something for which our psychology has no place. What sounds "interesting," when you are faced with it repeatedly in an undeniable and unavoidable way, can be downright traumatic. Violating the mind's paradigms of time, space, the very nature of reality and even the nature of identity (if you're the viewer), is no small thing. It is *destabilizing*. This requires psychological adaptation (in cycles), and the lack of ability to adapt is a large trench in the landscape that many (if not most) viewers fall into, occasionally or permanently – as humans have throughout time, in shamanic cultures. On the other side of that trench, you find people who are highly independent, unusually tenacious -- and who are profoundly changed by the experience.

RV is difficult to quantify. Even in science, it can only be measured *indirectly*, compared to chance. For the judge, they may see 4 or 5 options and choose the best data-match from those. But for the *viewer* it isn't compared to chance. There is no way to truly measure the chance of someone recording details and context out of literally a *universe* of possibilities.

A target could be a volcano or a tornado, or what's inside the trunk of a car. It could be Mars or a jungle or a giant squid. It could be the health of a cow or the environment of a hostage or the location of a lost key or someone skiing. It could be the detail of a technology or any event in the past, present or future. It could even be a concept, or other things which have validity but not 'physical mass.' When a target is done double-blind, it can be *anything*. It can often be not only anything in the world, but even *out of* this world. As large as a galaxy or as small as an atomic element. As nebulous as an idea or emotion, or as physical as an earth-mover of hardened steel. Any task number is random, and questions are 'generically standard' (usually common to most the viewer's tasks). There is no information at all given about the target.

Now when you consider all those possibilities, the fact that a viewer can still describe what even *seems* like the same thing as the hidden target is pretty amazing by any measure. This isn't a chance-guess of 1-in-5. It's like *information pulled out of infinity*. The fact that they are describing something even *like* the target is already an impressive feat of what we call *psi* (for lack of a better word).

16

Remote Viewing UFOS and The Visitors

The target "context" is something we usually know enough about to validate accuracy upon. That is one of several reasons why the double-blind element of the RV science protocol is so crucial: it is the only way we can take incredibly limited 'knowns,' and use them for at least that initial validation of "target contact" on the viewer's part. If a viewer is provably psychic enough to get that part of it down, it's easy to see why one might wish to treat seriously the details they go on to get within that context.

Indira Gandhi is quoted as having once said: "My father said there are two kinds of people in the world: those who do the work, and those who take the credit. *Try to be in the first group - There is less competition there.*" That is certainly the case for viewing. When you find someone "walking the talk" it is both rare and amazing. Watch for some time and you begin to realize this is the "tiny kernel of real" all that other drama and hype is based upon. All of culture's wishful thinking and delusion, all the money and manipulation, in the end most of it is smoke and mirrors: but for a tiny kernel of truth. That truth, up close, can shock and excite and upset anybody. Then it can free your mind *literally.*

Inside the niche-of-niche field that is Remote Viewing is a man who has been walking the talk and setting records since the first time he was ever 'tried' by science. A poor boy of Scot descent who grew up in Catholic schools and on the meaner streets of Florida in that era, he became an Army combat soldier, and lived through the middle of nearly every battle infamously named in the Vietnam-war era. He was assassinated years later overseas, but after dying, re-awoke on the table under the sheet the Austrian doctors had placed over him, babbling (he once said) about God and the White Light.

As it turns out, the Army didn't want to hear about God and the White Light, and sent him for a lot of exams to check out his brain and psychology. Failing to find anything wrong with him, and by this time he'd learned to be silent about all the interesting things in that experience and that had begun happening with him since, he simply went back to work. He was highly successful in his area of focus, and had no other plans until the day someone from a controversial black project experiment, scanning military records for people they theorized might be prone to psi talent based on certain indicators, found him.

He was (and still is) a very practical and intelligent man, trained in a much larger array of weapons than average, in shipbuilding and electronics, and many more things for his distinct MOS (military specialty). They briefed him about psi, and he was both very skeptical and yet, open-minded and curious, in great part because of his own experiences for which he had no easy explanation. They put him in the lab and gave him six trials to see if he could get even a few decent match sets. This means a judge ranking his data against 4-5 options to result in, they would hope, a 1st, 2nd or 3rd place match for each.

He got six out of six first-place matches. After some great angst over leaving his existing specialty, he decided that the amazing element of this, if real and it seemed to be, was both the greatest potential to man and the greatest threat to our country in the hands of enemies. He joined the black project and Joseph W. "Joe" McMoneagle officially became Viewer #001.

The existence of some of the RV projects funded by the US Government was made public in 1995 by the CIA for their own reasons. Those were not really the ones they publicly marketed and they provided some 'popcorn science' as a form of cover, plus there were several levels of complex politics and devious intent involved, but you know it's the CIA, what can you do. They made a point not to provide a signature that would keep the project's personnel from publicly talking about it. This resulted in some of the final unit's members going forth into public media as 'experts' offering their format (methodology) for sale and *defining* RV as if it were that method, rather than its science-derived protocol. This radically, drastically changed the information and model presented to the public about RV, probably in a way the CIA is happy about, but not in a way serious viewers would be. This has allowed an enormous amount of confusion, disinformation, fraud and disillusion ever since. On the bright side, the program going public did allow McMoneagle to publish a second edition of his book MIND TREK, which addressed the program he couldn't mention previously.

It is spring of 2015 as I write this. Recently a great deal of research documentation, which has been buried in file drawers and privacy for decades, has gone public in a couple of books released by Dr. Edwin C. May and in a huge papers collection. This is a great thing for the field of RV, which deserves to have that available to the public. Much of that work involves the viewing of Joseph McMoneagle.

Meanwhile, Viewer #001 has been steadily walking the road all along. When asked, Joe had difficulty remembering how many demonstrations he's done over the past nearly-40 years – *"many!"* - but he originally began doing them for a Senate Committee, which had a direct effect on the funding sources for the US Government projects for over twenty years.

He has done over sixty demonstrations on National Television in seven countries. He says he likes to think of his 14 two-hour specials in Japan (done over four and a half years) as a testament to what remote viewing can do. Watching these shows is fascinating. It paired Joe's viewing with investigators and an on-the-ground team that would run around showing people his sketches saying, "Have you seen a building that looks like this?" In some cases they literally followed driving and even walking directions - up the stairs, down this-many-doors – amazing. During those shows, Joe demonstrated finding missing people on camera while double-blind to their location. (Everybody was blind: These were "cold cases.") Of the twenty-eight people he looked for, he was successful in finding half, or fourteen people.

One of those people was missing more than thirty years, and Joe reported that he was *not* Japanese, but was actually *Korean*. That after he retired, he returned to Korea to live until he died six years earlier. He was then able to find half of his ashes buried in Pusan, South Korea; as well as half his ashes buried in Tokyo. Because of the records in Tokyo the studio discovered a Grand Uncle; so, his great grand-children were able to meet their Grand Uncle who informed them that no one in the family on either family side except his father and himself knew that he was Korean. He was adopted when he was only a few months old and brought to Japan and raised as Japanese. This is only one story -- most all of the viewings done for the Japanese projects have amazing stories as part of them (including the work when searching for many people who were not, at least publicly or at that time, found).

McMoneagle is the only viewer from the Star Gate program who has been working on the science research side while at the same time working as a full-time remote viewer. He's supported *hundreds* of clients and CEOs of industry for nearly 40 years at this point. He's worked with dozens of Police Commissioners, Police and Sheriff Captains as well as Detectives on a repetitive basis. He is also the *only* psychic in history who has become a full member of the Parapsychological Association by invitation, where he contributes considerable insight to the organization's efforts.

At this point in time, Joe has more documented science testing and experience than any psychic in the world. He has more documented double-blind "public demonstrations" than any psychic in the world. (There are psychics who do demos, but it's rarely a double-blind.) He has nearly four decades of military and other 'official agency' work which, for those done in an RV protocol (which existed [and only privately at first] a mere few years before he began), makes him the viewer with the most experience in *that* kind of applications work in the world also. There are a few good viewers out there; but in the larger scope, nobody in *his* league.

Other viewers (especially if they come through the commercial 'format' approaches) may be used to seeing sessions of many pages of simple descriptives and pieces that an analyst -- or feedback -- might be needed for deciphering into a whole. What you will see in Joe's viewing is a viewer who has contact, concept and context. Who can put all the data together into something you don't need to be an analyst (or a psychic) to figure out.

As a personal aside, Joe views not only the target, but often as a point of humour any match-decoys as well, tasker intent, feedback and more, for the larger context. He has amazed many people he's done viewing for by sketching (sometimes on a napkin!) the other 'secret potential targets' also. This is what comes of developing your own internal path and format over the long term, and holding fiercely to the science-derived protocol elements that are critical to helping shape the fairly unique psychology needed for developing serious skill.

All of Joe's work is done double-blind to the tasking focus. (In some media work, sometimes the tasking 'context' is known, e.g.

that he is looking for the location of a person. But the location, the actual target, is not known to anybody.) He provides the project manager his results and there is no initial feedback in case there is retasking. If retasking happens, it is based on the data he already provided, so 'retasking' questions are specific to that data.

He is no-nonsense about viewing, making a point to be very clear about what falls within an RV protocol and what is outside it. One of his books, 'Remote Viewing Secrets,' is almost entirely dedicated to fleshing out and explaining protocol for viewers. In part because this is the area that the modern commercial field of formats-for-sale has done the most damage in. And in part because it is the most important fundamental, supporting the actual viewing as an art that viewers need to understand and employ for their own good.

People often exclaim when they see his work -- in impressed awe or in rejection when they just can't believe it could be possible. It's possible. Every alphabet soup agency in the US Government knows it's possible and has hired him at some point. He's getting older now and he wants to do other things with his time, like art and sculpture for example. Or when viewing, doing so for projects of his own interest. Sometimes, though less now, he still views for hire.

And on very rare occasion, some curious altruist like Tunde Atunrase will come along and say: *Why is nobody looking into these fascinating things?!* And out of their own pocket they will hire him to view targets they want to know the truth about. If we're lucky, they'll also be viewers, like Tunde, so they will have a good eye for what we *do* have some information about -- which in a double-blind means a degree of confirmation that the viewer is on-target. I don't even want to ask how much he spent on the work that went into this book, though I know it took a long time to gather the information and write. We all owe Tunde a big thanks for making the effort not just for his own curiosity, but on behalf of everybody else's interest also.

Viewers like McMoneagle bring home the potential of psi as an opportunity, and as a threat. Some of the sessions I have seen by Joe over time have had a degree of detail that leaves one lost for words. When you see what he can really do, you understand why such a man would give up everything he'd worked for in his own military specialty to dive a hard left onto the path of a far-out fringe-black project, just because its potential was so profound. And you get an idea why the result of seeing some of this work up-close can lead to a visit to a bar for "eight martinis," as intelligence members labelled the more *reality-cracking* session work.

It must be said that nobody is perfect. Joe's success rate is around 88% last I heard him mention it -- he has been measured by the science lab as well as by the overall stats of other demonstrations for nearly four decades. (There are usually two numbers: one for assumed target 'contact' and another for accuracy of measurable details within that.) That doesn't just mean he has that much chance of a judge matching his data to one of five options. For him, in a double-blind, it means the chance of picking details *out of a pool the size of the universe.*

Tunde Atunrase has put together a fascinating book about anomalies -- and about viewing on them -- that features a number of Joe's sessions (and some others, including his own). It's a fabulous contribution to the Viewing field, which is always in need of more documented double-blind viewing. (These targets lack most *feedback* for protocol, but the double-blind and base context for *some* feedback at least gives us something to go on, and he chose targets with as much context as possible - excellent choices.) It's an even more unique contribution to the Ufology field, which has had

23

more and heavier disinformation and strategic-deception efforts imposed upon it than any other topic in history. Often through *official* sources. That field needs a hard dose of truth from *any* source it can find.

If you want to know the truth about something, to whatever metaphysical degree truth can be objective – because there may be symbolic variance between all our subjective realities, even in 'real-life' never mind in viewing -- it's a good bet that McMoneagle could tell you. As Tunde learned, almost the hard way, be sure you really want to *know* before you ask!

Because when Joe views, *he really views*. His sessions are often sit-down-and-have-a-drink amazing. So sit down and have a drink, and prepare yourself for some very interesting -- and very *controversial* -- insights into some famous (and infamous) "anomalous claims."

-- PJ Gaenir, May 2015

CHAPTER 1

EXTRA-SENSORY PERCEPTION:
The Early Years

"I never liked to get into debates with the skeptics, because if you didn't believe that remote viewing was real, you hadn't done your homework."

- **Major General Edmund R Thompson**, U.S. Army Assistant Chief of Staff for Intelligence, 1977-81, Deputy Director for Management and Operations, DIA, 1982-84[1]

For as long as I can remember I have always been fascinated by the workings of the human mind. Over the years, I have been exposed to various teachings, books and other scholarly works that have tried to unravel the mysteries of how our minds work. It's been a slow journey and I have had to endure a lot of detours along the way towards understanding and unlocking the secrets of consciousness.

We still have a long way to go before science can explain some of the things you are about to read in this book, but it is hoped the reader will approach the subject with an open mind and perhaps explore some of the findings presented here and continue with their own investigations.

Do we all possess latent *super powers* within our own minds?

Can a human being, using nothing but their mind, accurately perceive unknown or hidden individuals, objects, and far distant locations, outside of normal space/time constrictions as we understand them today? The answer according to science as demonstrated across laboratories across the globe, suggest that we do.

We are capable of creating wonderful dreams as well as terrible nightmares. We can create and destroy both with equal measure. There is no end to our individual and collective human potential, but just what exactly can we do? How far can we push the boundaries of what we know about consciousness? How much are we ready to accept, and ultimately validate, when it comes to unravelling the true potential of our minds?

Mainstream science tells us we are no more than just independent carbon based, brain driven, biological automations naturally evolved for survival and basic breeding on this planet.

However, there are a small, yet growing number of scientists who, over the decades, have successfully demonstrated under stringent scientific protocols, as well as highly classified government funded projects, that humans are far more complex creatures than we ever imagined. On top of known basic sensory perceptions such as sight, sound, hearing, taste and touch, there exists another form of perception *some* brave scientists are slowly coming to terms with.

It's called Extra-Sensory Perception.

The aim of this book is primarily to showcase a selected range of real world examples and applications of an off-shoot of ESP called Remote Viewing. For this reason, a lot of the early history of this field - and there is quite a bit of it - will be limited to its standard history which is varied, and often disputed amongst researchers. I will try however to offer a very brief timeline of its origins and refer the reader to more specialized historical references.

Remote Viewing was born out of the early scientific research into the study of Extra-Sensory Perception (ESP). There were probably hundreds of individuals associated with the development and research into ESP over the years and its parent field, Parapsychology, which is the scientific study of paranormal activity.

The first recorded examples in telepathy (picture drawing) experiments began as far back as 1882 right here in London at the Society for Psychical Research. The trials were undertaken by George Albert Smith and his colleague Douglas Blackburn. According to pioneer remote viewer and acclaimed artist, the legendary Ingo Swann, Smith and Douglas caused quite a stir when their 'psychic' drawings were published to cries of cheating and disbelief which according to Swann proved to be unfounded. Further research into these early psychic drawings continued slowly and under much skepticism from the scientific community of that time. Their findings over the years showed test participants consistently performed *better* than chance. Eventually other notable researchers began to arrive on the scene. One such individual was René Warcollier author of the book, *Mind To Mind*.

In June 1946, Warcollier gave a lecture at the world renowned Collège de Sorbonne in Paris. He presented his ground breaking findings on *Telepathic Experiments* spanning a period of almost 40 years and according to today's leading experts in remote viewing, most of his research laid the ground work for future scientific protocols incorporated into various PSI experiments even to this day.

Across the Atlantic, the Americans started getting involved in psi research with the publication of *Mental Radio*, a book published by Upton Sinclair and his wife Mary Sinclair about their own experiences with what was known back then as *Thought Transference* and today widely referred to as Telepathy. They would isolate themselves, and attempt to send thoughts or mental images to each other often with miles of space between them. Their results proved rather successful and captured the imagination of fellow researchers worldwide.

Another one of those early pioneers back in the 1930's was JB Rhine, who along with his wife, Louisa, at Duke University in North Carolina USA, came up with the term Parapsychology, which was the study of various forms of psychic activity such as telepathy. They developed the Zener Card Test featuring various symbols, which would require a designated 'sender' who would focus on one of the cards, while a 'receiver' would try and guess correctly what card the sender was focusing on, all done under blind scientific controlled settings.

These were the early days of parapsychology's humble and painstaking beginnings. The subject was often treated with scorn and ridicule within the wider scientific community, with little or no funding for the few brave souls who dared to challenge the prevailing paradigms of the time. All that was about to change when in the early 1970's, alarming stories began to reach intelligence agencies in the U.S.A involving cold war enemies, the Soviet Union, taking a little bit more than just a passing interests in PSI phenomenon.

A new era was about to begin and the art of war had now shifted from the domain of the battlefield into more exotic territory…

…The Human Mind.

Remote Viewing UFOS and The Visitors

Remote Viewing's most significant research began in one of America's most prestigious scientific think tanks, The **Stanford Research Institute** now known simply as **SRI International**. In 1972, a bright physicist by the name of Hal Puthoff headed a team of dedicated researchers and test subjects, early on adding another scientist, Russell Targ, to investigate ESP and the new soviet threat.

The psychic arms race had begun.

The initial project was funded by The Central Intelligence Agency **(CIA)** to the tune of $50,000.

Ingo Swann, an artist and gifted psychic from New York, was making waves at the American Society for Psychical Research (ASPR) around the same time with his psychic feats and psycho-energetic experiments. Swann was eventually drafted into the SRI project, and together with Puthoff, they started their Remote Viewing experiments using the game-changing remote viewing protocol that would shake the world of parapsychology to its core.

Other participants in this project, who also contributed immensely to the creation and establishment of the RV Protocols, included Keith Harary, Duane Elgin, Pat Price, Gary Langford and Hella Hammid. The Project eventually ended in 1975.

Another important contributor to the science behind remote viewing, Ed May, joined the SRI team in 1976, and later became its program director. In 1991, the project was transferred to The Science Applications International Corporation (SAIC) under May.

There were many more contributors, but this is only a brief introduction to the history of RV and the reader is advised to check the bibliography appended to this book for further in depth historical references to the complete origins of Remote Viewing.

CHAPTER 2

Top Secret Classified Remote Viewing Military Intelligence Operations

"There were times when they wanted to push buttons and drop bombs on the basis of our information"[2]

- **Dr. Hal Puthoff** ,
  Former Operations
  Manager of the remote
  viewing program

Based on the ongoing success and continued funding of Remote Viewing projects by the CIA-backed SRI team, operations swiftly moved into the real world of espionage, starting with The US Army's INSCOM first operational Remote Viewing Unit under the code name *'Gondola Wish'* from 1977 – 1979.

Other Top secret and highly classified remote viewing projects soon followed:

- *Project **Grill Flame** - Army INSCOM/AMSAA 1979-1983*

- *Project **Center Lane** - Army INSCOM/AMSAA 1983 – 1985*

- *Project **Dragoon Absorb** - Army INSCOM and CIA 1985-1986*

- *Project **Sun Streak** – Defence Intelligence Agency (DIA) 1986 – 1990*

- *Project **Star Gate** – Started by the DIA and ended up with the CIA 1990 - 1995*

Remote Viewing UFOS and The Visitors

By the end of June 1995, the last U.S. operational Remote Viewing Program, Project Star Gate, was closed by the CIA. However, the story did not end there. Due to a series of what some have called deliberate leaks mixed with claims and counter-claims of the activities of these classified state-run psychic programs, there was a gradual, yet steady release of information into the public domain.

I first heard about Remote Viewing through a British Channel 4 documentary back in 1995 called, **"The Real X- Files: America's Psychic Spies"**. I recall sitting alone in my flat at the time in Clapham, South London, watching in complete disbelief, the revelations of a secret group of trained military psychics spying on the likes of Saddam Hussein and captured hostages in Iran. I watched in amazement as the writer and narrator of the documentary, Jim Schnabel, interviewed many of the participants in the various military RV programs, and even watched as he attempted an actual demonstration of Remote Viewing himself. *[World-famous UK crop circle researcher Colin Andrews has implied that Jim Schnabel was employed by the CIA.*]*

'Surely this sort of thing can't be real, and even if it was, wouldn't we have heard about it on the news?' I thought to myself. As it turned out and unbeknown to me at the time, Remote Viewing was already a major talking point in the United States.

News of the top-secret psi programs started reaching the media in quantity back in 1988 after former U.S. military viewers began to retire one by one from their units. One of those viewers was a Major Ed Dames (*Retired*) who would later become famous on various U.S. radio networks, in particular the Coast to Coast AM with Art Bell syndicated radio show as the voice of 'Doom' or Dr Doom due to his predictions of doom and terror. The airwaves were filled with tales of invading aliens and UFOs as well as offering the public, for a small fee, the chance to use psychic powers to save themselves, and their spouse and children from the doom he was predicting eventually moving onto selling videos and later DVD's from 1997 with the promise they too could become just like him, a psychic spy.

There are those who believe the sudden release of classified Remote Viewing projects, may have been done deliberately under a well-orchestrated and planned campaign of disinformation, to prepare for the inevitable awkward questions and subsequent media circus that would follow, as the last surviving classified RV program, Project Star Gate, was terminated for good.

The CIA, which since 1972 had funded this extraordinary research to the tune of (and perhaps even beyond) **$20,000,000,00 US dollars** for over **22 years,** now suddenly wanted absolutely *nothing* to do with psychic espionage and released a highly controversial study declaring their own RV programs more or less a failure.

Yet here lies the irony. If it was such a failure, why was each program consistently provided funding, under extremely hostile pressure from hard-line anti-PSI Army intel and countless Oversight Committees, whose members before 'signing off' on what became millions in funding, often demanded proven past results, oversight-committee demonstrations, and other justification before funding was granted?

This is a very important question the reader should bear in mind, and proves the Remote Viewing Programs and early SRI research, DID indeed work and work very well otherwise funding would have stopped many years ago.

As for the highly controversial CIA report on the reasons why it cancelled the Star Gate program, this was finally laid to rest after the recent release of thousands of previously classified documents via the FOIA *Freedom of information Act,* which showed irrefutable evidence in support of the various remote viewing projects from virtually all sectors of the intelligence communities.

Over the years, many of the world's leading parapsychology experts also presented findings refuting any claims that classified research and projects were unsuccessful, and to the contrary, demonstrating just how impressively successful the investigative efforts and testing had actually been. Luminaries such as Dean Radin, Richard Broughton, Charles T. Tart, Professor Jessica Uttis, Dr Jean Millay, Stephan A. Schwartz, Ingo Swann, Russell Targ to name a few. Most recently Dr Edwin C. May, along with Co-author Sonali Bhatt Marwaha published *Anomalous Cognition – Remote Viewing Research and Theory* which I highly recommend to anyone still in doubt as to the reality of PSI. The book offers a look at some of the definitive evidence as defined by today's best scientific minds on the topic.

CHAPTER 3

What is Remote Viewing?

So what exactly was this strange method of psychic espionage? A method or tool wrapped up in complete secrecy and utilized by virtually all arms of the US intelligence Services for so many years? Remote Viewing was developed out of the combined research of early ESP studies including psychic or telepathic picture drawing experiments covered in the previous chapter.

Remote Viewing (RV) is the ability to perceive and communicate accurate information about places, people, concepts or events, under an appropriately **'blind'** protocol, without regard to distance, space or time.

In a **'double blind'** protocol, the person attempting to do the remote viewing has no idea whatsoever what he or she is viewing until *after* he or she reports findings, and only then is the target made known to the remote viewer.

Two other crucial requirements must also be met before any form of remote viewing can be said to have occurred:

1. **The remote viewing must be planned in advance.**

2. **There must be verifiable feedback to judge the level of accuracy of what has been psychically viewed.**

It is important to elaborate on the protocol once again:

The remote viewer is given absolutely NO information whatsoever about a planned target. The Remote Viewer uses <u>nothing</u> but his mind and working alone, attempts to describe the target that has been assigned to him or her. In certain instances others may be present during the actual remote viewing, but no one in the same room must have access to the target information.

Why the strong emphasis on the protocol? Well without the protocol there can be no remote viewing. A solid double-blind Remote Viewing protocol is what sets this particular form of psychic functioning apart from the rest of the "ESP" world and its history, both in science and in culture. What we call "an RV protocol" is a group of rules scientifically developed to ascertain whether a successful demonstration of psychic functioning has occurred. *(If a double-blind protocol is performed by a viewer working alone, in the layman's world this is sometimes called **solo-blind**.)*.

The RV protocol is the *primary* difference between the claims and use of mediums, spiritualists, tarot reading, astrology, palmistry and other similar tools of psychic functioning. This is not to say the above methods do not work, or are inferior in any way compared to remote viewing. I have personally met some amazingly talented individuals over the years who use some of these tools successfully. The only difference between all these methods is the successful application of an appropriate RV protocol.

In Remote Viewing, the protocol encompasses *every* aspect of the experiment. The details can vary, but there are several **points of RV Protocol** that are always expected to be followed:

Planned and Aimed

The psychic session must be planned and done on purpose. If you get a "spontaneous insight" or have a dream, that is not Remote Viewing. RV is when you *intend* to collect information about a specific target.

Double-Blind

In most experiments, if the person giving the answers does not know the question, but someone in the room or in any contact with them does, it would be called "blind" or "single-blind". **Remote Viewing is required to be "double-blind"**. That means there are two (double) layers of "blinding". It means the psychic cannot know the target, AND, nobody else who is present with the psychic during the session (even by remote means such as webcam or phone) can know the target either. This is because even pheromones, voice-frequencies, and many other "invisible" physiological senses can transfer information below the conscious level.

Solo Blind

If a psychic (viewer) is working alone and does not know the target, we call this **"solo blind"**. This is not the same as "single-blind," which implies someone with the viewer did know the target (that would be out of protocol). Solo blind just means the 'double' is "not applicable," because the viewer was alone in the room from start to finish.

Feedback

Although you can be psychic about anything (the future, for example), in order to "validate" the data IS psychic and not just a wild guess, it has to be at least partly correct. In order to know what is correct, we need the real info to 'compare to' the session data. We call that info "feedback." For example, a target could be a building, and a photograph could be taken of the building. The instructions to the viewer might say, "Describe the focus of the photo at the time the photo was taken." The "feedback" would be the photograph. This photo would help the viewer (and any judge or scientist) evaluate how much of the viewer's information is accurate. If you are viewing offline, a target could also be a future event, or your experience of visiting a nearby location. In online viewing, most things are photos and/or text or brief video clips.[3]

Unfortunately, many claim to teach and do remote viewing without any understanding of these basic protocols, or worse, confuse the RV protocol with a Remote Viewing *Method*. The two are completely different and need to be understood before we proceed any further.

Methods Vs Protocols

The Protocol

As previously mentioned, the Remote Viewing Protocol is what defines Remote Viewing. As a result, anyone claiming to be remote viewing must follow the strict protocols surrounding properly-blinded procedures, as well as the availability of feedback, if they wish to be taken seriously. These elements are required to determine the accuracy of information, and the solely viewer-sourced nature of its provision, in order to say we have evidence that psychic functioning has indeed taken place.

If you come across examples of remote viewing, or claims of remote viewing, good or bad, or by anyone - including stage magicians, skeptics or debunkers, always demand to see whether proper protocol, as described above, has been followed. Viewers who take protocol seriously will volunteer such information as part of their work, because they *know* it is important, and because it is important to them, too. If you have to interrogate someone to get the details of their protocol, or if they don't mention it, it's usually a clue to their real operation.

The Remote Viewing examples and cases you will read in this book all - *without exception* - follow this fundamental double or solo blind protocol and where there is still lack of complete feedback in some of these examples, this is always explained up front.

The Method

How you "do" your remote viewing is commonly known as your format or your methodology. You can use any method of your choice, whether it's reading cards, praying, meditating, lucid dreaming, crystal balls, whatever floats your boat can be your preferred method of remote viewing. However from a historical point of view, several methods have emerged since remote viewings declassification. These methods have been introduced to the public via private training and tutoring by former ex-military remote viewers over the years and often used successfully.

One of these structured methods originated from Ingo Swann back in the SRI days (1980s), it was called **Controlled Remote Viewing** or **Coordinate Remote Viewing** (CRV)

Since the declassification of this method, and thanks mainly to the U.S. Military Remote Viewers such as Joe McMoneagle, Paul Smith, Ed Dames, Lyn Buchanan and David Morehouse, some of whom were originally taught CRV by Ingo Swann, the general public, have for many years now been exposed to CRV and its many derivatives such as Technical Remote Viewing (TRV), Scientific Remote Viewing (SRV) and (TDS) Trans-Dimensional Remote Viewing to name a few.

How does Remote Viewing Work?

It is beyond the scope of this book or even my expertise to go in-depth into how or even why Remote Viewing works, however, the common theoretical belief is that RV falls with the domain of quantum mechanics and consciousness. I would recommend the serious student of remote viewing to read up on the works of Ed May Ph.D, Ingo Swann, Hal Puthoff, Jean Millay Ph.D, Jessica Utts Ph.D, Stephan Schwartz, Paul H. Smith Ph.D, Angela Thompson Smith Ph.D, Russell Targ and many other brilliant minds who have contributed to the further understanding, research and science behind remote viewing over the years.

A more simplified view on how RV works, and one I personally appreciate due to its simplicity, comes from Joe McMoneagle :

"Simply put, I think that I am sending myself information from the future. In other words, at some point in the future, I will come to know the answer to whatever question has been put to me in the past. Therefore, *whenever* the information is passed to me in its **accurate** form, that is when I send it back to myself in the past"[4]

Another popular theory is that ALL information, past present and future is connected in a quantum matrix like field and accessible via consciousness.

CHAPTER 4

Joseph W. McMoneagle

"A good remote viewer, operating under the stringent controls established within a qualified laboratory, could put such potentials within easy reach of those bold enough to take advantage"

- Joseph McMoneagle,
  MIND TREK

There were however, other methods employed prior to the introduction of Swann's CRV methodology. Talented viewers such as Pat Price, Hella Hammid, Keith Harary and even the world famous and controversial Israeli psychic, Uri Geller, all demonstrated astounding psychic feats under strict laboratory conditions involving Remote Viewing, using their own unique psychic abilities which we all possess to some degree or another. One of the greatest viewers of our time would emerge from this natural group of talented SRI viewers, and is today wildly acknowledged as probably the world's best remote viewer.

His name is Joseph McMoneagle.

Joseph W. McMoneagle was born January 10, 1946. He joined the U.S. Army and ended up doing classified operations for the Army Security Agency. From 1964 – 1978 he was assigned to various overseas missions all over the world before ending up at the U.S. Army Intelligence and Security Command (INSCOM) in Arlington, Virginia. Due to a number of highly unusual events in Joe's life such as a near death experience and spontaneous out-of-body incidences he was recruited into the previously discussed and highly classified Star Gate remote viewing program.

As a result of the remarkable work he accomplished during the program he was awarded the highly distinguished **Legion Of Merit** award for providing critical intelligence reported at the highest echelons of the U.S. military and Government, including agencies such as the DEA, CIA, NSA, DIA and the Joint Chief Of staff producing crucial and vital intelligence unavailable from any other source. Joe retired from the Army in 1984 but continues to provide Remote Viewing services via his company Intuitive intelligence Agency (IIA) based in Virginia.

He has successfully demonstrated remote viewing on television around the world live and filmed more than half a dozen times. He has demonstrated on shows such as Put To The Test, an ABC TV Special; Mysteries of the Mind, a Reader's Digest Special; numerous appearances on the Paranormal World of Paul McKenna, which was shown on Channel Four in London, England; eight "Psychic Detective" episodes currently showing on various SKY channels (and two "Joe McMoneagle" episodes) for Nippon Television in Japan which can be found online via YouTube.

Joe currently teaches an *Introduction to Remote Viewing* course at The Monroe Institute (TMI) In Virginia US. He also has over 30 years' experience as a professional remote viewer which was primarily why I picked him to work some of the more *advanced* enigma operational type targets and cases you are about to read in the book. Joe's remarkable abilities and talent as a remote viewer for his country during military service and decades of successful laboratory research trials, can best be described in the following two examples:

1979 Declassified Remote Viewing of a Top Secret Soviet Nuclear Submarine Base in Severodvinsk (Russia)

One of Remote Viewings most remarkable success stories documented and verified was the successful viewing of a previously unheard of Soviet type Typhoon Nuclear submarine in September 1979.

Joe, at the time, was assigned to the classified remote viewing program called **Project Grill Flame**. One of the very first operational targets handed to the project was a mysterious and unknown building located in Severodvinsk, behind the iron curtain of the former Soviet Union. American Intelligence agencies, and specifically, the NSC and OACSIDA - *Office of the Assistant Chief of Staff for Intelligence Department of the Army,* were desperate to find out what was going on at the location. Having totally exhausted all other forms of intelligence gathering tools, they decided to turn to the psychic spooks at Grill Flame to see what they might come up with.

Joe was given nothing more than geographic coordinates of the target and with no further information, proceeded to describe in his mind what he *perceived* at the location.

Joe began to describe a large industrial type building, located in a vast cold wasteland of ice and rock, within this wasteland; he described a huge shed-like building. He then went on to describe the ongoing construction of a gigantic nuclear submarine, the likes of which he had never seen before or heard of. He drew in great detail the sub, its launch tubes, and how it was being constructed.

The results were handed back to the NSC (National Security Council) but they dismissed Joe's report out of hand expecting instead to find what they believed at the time, was just another Soviet assault ship and certainly not a submarine of the size and capabilities Joe had clearly described.

One of those who dismissed the data out of hand was Robert Gates who would later become the Deputy Director of the CIA.

As a result, Joe did another remote viewing session on the target, again verifying what he initially perceived but this time he could see the sub would be launched and in operational use *within the next 4 months!*

This time the intelligence community took notice.

As a direct result of Joe's predictions, the NSC arranged for overhead satellite photographs to be taken of the area on September 28, 1980. What they saw completely blew their minds. In clear detail, just as Joe had predicted, was the image of a gigantic submarine no one had seen before thus validating with accurate feedback, the entire remote viewing operation from start to finish. Joe was to go on and further demonstrate the same level of skill and service using RV for his country for many years to come, eventually earning him the prestigious *Legion of Merit Award.*

The reader can learn more about this case and see the detailed drawings and full transcript of the Severodvinsk Remote Viewing session for the first time in a newly published book, *ESP WARS East & West by Ed May PhD, Victor Rubel PhD and loyd Auerbach M.S.*

Lawrence Livermore Laboratory
Remote Viewing Example:

Another stunning example of Joe McMoneagle's remote viewing skills took place on 8th May 1987, and was part of a series of four classified Remote Viewing trials at the request of the U.S. Air Force and conducted under the supervision of Edwin May PhD.

The trial would involve sending out an individual from the agency sponsoring the RV trial (*the Air Force*), as a live human beacon to specific targets of a technological nature. The objective was to see if a remote viewer could describe the beacons location at a given time in detail. Under the tightest of laboratory conditions, and ensuring the viewer and those around him had no access to the locations, the 24 hour trials went ahead as planned within the San Francisco Bay area, between 2200 hours and 0800 hours the following morning.

A representative from the air force approached Ed May and informed him he would be at two undisclosed sites. He would visit the first site at 10am and the next site at Noon. At approximately 10am that morning, Joe was instructed to view the location and whereabouts of the individual from the air force, described in RV terms as *the beacon*.

Joe described the target in detail as being a large research and development facility and said the beacon was walking around an "unusual T - shaped building with 6 floors covered with glass"[5] As it turned out that was EXACTLY where the beacon was. He was at the Lawrence Livermore Laboratory; a nuclear research facility, fifty miles east of SRI. Joe produced just one drawing for this target as shown on the next page. You can also see the T-shaped building including the correct number of floors six in total.

As a side note Joe also accurately described all four target sites in uncanny accuracy. The results of these trials impressed the CIA as well as the Air Force especially when you consider the fact Joe had never visited these sites before and yet accurately describes the locations in high detail.

Would Joe's highly skilled ability and 30 plus years of remote viewing expertise prove valuable when applied to targets of an extreme nature?

Lawrence Livermore Nuclear Laboratory – Notice the T-shaped Admin building top left side of the picture.

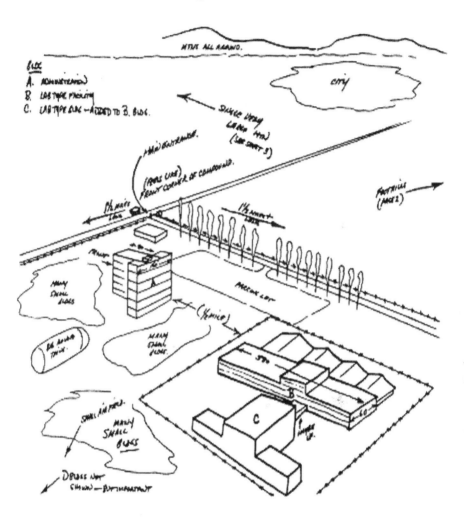

Joe McMoneagle's 1987 Remote Viewing Sketch of a declassified outbounder experiment sponsored by the U.S. Air force/CIA. Also notice the T-Shaped Admin Building - with correct number of floors - where the beacon was located at the time of the remote viewing session. Note also the row of trees corresponding to the actual photo.

Joseph W. McMoneagle

Remote Viewer #001

CHAPTER 5

How it all started - My Introduction to RV

"I can promise you that learning RV will change you. Your world view will change. Your priorities will change, and many things about you will change. These changes will begin shortly after you begin training."

- **Bill Ray** [Former U.S. Intelligence member of Project Star Gate]

My interest in remote viewing began back in 1995, but it would take another six years before I took some form of structured training which I had always dreamed of. It was a time of much apprehension and uncertainty not just on a global level but a personal one as well.

October 2002 - Osama Bin Laden's backed terror group, Al Qaeda, had unleashed hell on American soil the previous year, heralding a new age of international global terrorism the likes of which the world had never seen. I had been following various dedicated RV forums on the internet for a few years and desperately wanted to learn what the US Military had been secretly doing for so many years.

I wanted to learn how to be a *psychic spy.*

Times were hard back then, trying to hold a job while supporting a small family. I just could not afford the fees some ex US military remote viewers were charging, plus the time to fly over and attend courses halfway across the globe was never going to happen at that time.

That would all change when a professional remote viewer, by the name of Pru Calabrese, offered to teach me RV in one of her classes here in the UK. Pru was a second generation Remote Viewer who lived and worked in Carlsbad, California in the US.

I had known Pru for some time online for a few years and we communicated briefly from time to time.

She was trained by Dr Courtney Brown, a mathematician and social scientist who at the time taught in the Department of Political Science at Emory University in Atlanta, Georgia. Courtney was originally trained by Major Ed Dames, one of Ingo Swann's CRV students and a veteran of the U.S. Army's final RV program, Project Star Gate.

She worked with Courtney Brown in 1995 at his Farsight Institute and was trained in all stages of Courtney's SRV (Scientific Remote Viewing) methodology. She left Farsight after the infamous and tragic Hale Bopp incident, when a Los Angeles religious cult called Heaven's Gate, committed ritual suicide based on their misguided belief the Hale-Bopp comet of 1997, was harbouring an alien space craft or *beings* that would rendezvous with Earth, allowing the cult to hitch – a - ride to God knows where.

It was believed by many in the public that the cult was influenced by the information broadcasted on a popular US late-night radio show, Coast to Coast AM with Art Bell. *(This is disputed by some, who say the information, as well as the initial report from an amateur astronomer which sparked it, merely validated what they already believed.)* Courtney and Pru claimed their team of viewers, from Courtney's Farsight Institute, had indeed identified an unknown *'companion'* alongside the Hale-Bopp comet. As it turned out, no such companion was discovered scientifically, and in the wake of the tragic suicides, both Pru and Courtney were vilified. It is safe to say

50

it was not one of the remote viewing community's finest moments and this case, more than any other, highlights the dangers of making claims using remote viewing against targets that do not have full feedback but more importantly, as demonstrated in the Hale-Bopp incident, the consequences of failing to follow the **blind** rules as laid out in the Remote Viewing Protocols.

Pru eventually left Farsight and went on to form her own company, determined to learn from the mistakes made at Farsight, she turned her hands at professional remote viewing for a living. Her new venture was called *Transdimensional Systems* **(TDS)** based in Carlsbad, Los Angeles. By all accounts it looked like she was doing very well indeed.

The UK Sunday Times Magazine ran a seven page article in November, 2002 about TDS. The Sunday Times had sent a crew and a reporter, Tony Barrell to investigate Pru and her Company and find out if remote viewing was for real and whether it could be put to use for things such as the *war on terror*. The team worked a target he gave them and were successful. I followed her company's progress keenly and when an opportunity finally came up in October 2002 to train with her for several days, there would be no hesitation on my part.

Training Begins

They say once you take RV seriously, or take up training in a structured method; it changes your life completely. I'm not so sure about that, but I did leave that three day course with a sense of awe and accomplishment. It is true you do see the world in a somewhat different light that is hard to describe unless you've been exposed to similar consciousness expanding events or training programs such as those offered by The Monroe Institute (TMI) in Virginia.

As usual, I was late, and sheepishly entered the class to be greeted by Pru, who was pleasantly surprised I had turned up.

The course went well. It was fun, serious and educational, all at the same time. In hindsight, there were some things I probably would have questioned today regarding protocol awareness, but as this was a training course it did not matter that much. There were about 15 of us I think who attended the training.

Pru said she had to limit the number of requests, as she was inundated with people who wanted to do the course. One thing I noticed was the diversity of the group. Pru would later admit she did not randomly pick the attendees but wanted a diverse mix of individuals. What the specific criteria was, I do not know, but we all seemed to get along well.

We worked target after target, slowly getting a handle on the TDS RV methodology. I don't think I had done so much hand writing in a single class since my college days learning software engineering.

Pru brought along a former member of her company, who offered to assist with the training course. Another ex-employee of TDS, we were told, could not make it, but might be available the following day, which indeed turned out to be the case. During breaks, we listened in awe to what these former employees had to say about their adventures with TDS during their time there. One of the more sensational claims corroborated by the two men were the surveillance and spying by unknown U.S. Intelligence agencies on TDS staff. It got so bad one of the guys had to leave altogether and head back to Ireland where he came from.

I have since spoken to other former TDS members who backed up these claims. Hopefully the whole truth behind TDS and its demise will be revealed. Until then, it's impossible to verify some of the stories I have heard over the years.

The training continued, and we were promised a prize at some point for the best session for the following target. I could not remember the last time I actually won something in any class but I discovered my luck was about to change.

During our training, Pru knew what the target was but **never** told the students anything. We were blind and given nothing but random coordinate reference numbers which were called out by Pru.

"7382 – HGHD"

Her voice boomed out, as we started writing down our impressions of what the target was.

Pru promised us the student with the best data which matched the target, a special prize. So we all had an incentive to do well this time, which unfortunately for me, meant extra pressure. With my eye on the prize, I buckled down and got on with the task. I cleared my mind, remained focused, and began my ideogram drill as instructed. By the end of the session, I was certain nothing would make sense and convinced myself I had written a load of garbage. I thought to myself, "why would Pru give us a bland *'fireworks'* display with so many coloured lights and explosions and people dancing or being happy and filled with joy? It just *felt* like I was at

The BIGGEST party you could imagine.

I felt joyous, happy, elated, like someone was celebrating a birthday or anniversary. I even drew sketches of *fireworks* going off in all directions, as I *'observed'* the display from a distance. It really did *feel* like the mother of all parties very similar to those opening ceremonies in big stadiums or concerts with elaborate lights and fireworks everywhere.

I think we were given about 30 minutes to complete the session. I was dreading what Pru would reveal for our feedback but at the same time excited to at least find out what the target was all about. Pru and the trainer went round the class and inspected the sessions we did, not giving anything away, but focusing on making sure we were following the strict TDS remote viewing structure or method. Eventually she reached for an envelope, opened it, and revealed the target:

"Describe the Universe at the moment of its Creation"

To most of us, the birth of the universe is generally referred to as the Big Bang although this is often disputed amongst cosmologists. The class gasped in wonder and smiles as we all started talking at once at what we had sketched and described in our data. I must admit, I was pretty impressed with my data as it all began to make sense to me. The explosions, the spectacular firework display, the birthday celebrations and party-like *feeling* and atmosphere.

In retrospect, thirteen years after doing this particular training target, I often find myself smiling about the session because technically from a RV standpoint, there is no feedback for what *really* happened at the precise moment the universe was created. Without verifiable feedback no full remote viewing can be claimed to have taken place according to the strict RV protocol remote viewers must adhere to.

*[Also the trainer knew what the target was and I have to concede the possibility of subliminal transference of info real or imagined even though Pru never revealed a thing about the nature of the target. However since this was a training target it did not seem to matter at the time.]**

Yet there I was, completely ecstatic to have described what scientists or some scientist would call the big bang. At that moment in time, I didn't really care about protocol all I knew was I had just possibly described the moment the universe was born.

Pru must have agreed, because I won the first prize--although, funnily enough, I don't recall what that the prize was. I think it might have been a signed copy of her autobiography, or a Hemi-Sync CD like the ones we used for meditation prior to beginning a remote viewing session. I would later learn other students who had done the same target got similar data, including one lady who thought she was viewing her *own children* and was worried or concerned how they would cope in the big outside world along with *very strong* maternal feelings.

Could this be a reference to God/The Creator/The Source of ALL things worrying or caring about *its children* and creations as the universe expands?

Others described and mentioned numerous references to space, galaxies, planets, stars and so on.

I went home that first day of training with so many thoughts running through my head. It was all real. Remote Viewing actually does work.

Like any typical teacher, Pru could not resist giving the class some homework which I must admit I'm never too keen on, but didn't mind on this occasion. The task we were given was to set up a

verifiable target of our choice and we would then be paired with each other the following day, and take turns in monitoring, as well as viewing each other's targets.

For my target, I picked the famous site of Silbury Hill near Avebury in Wiltshire, a lovely land mark right here in England. I found a photo of the site and placed it an envelope ready for tomorrows training.

The next day, we found ourselves in a different room, somewhat smaller, but one that suited the class much better. As usual, in any classroom I happen to find myself in, I always prefer to sit at the back which in my school days wasn't the smartest thing to do if you were short sighted as I am, but old habits die hard I guess. Sitting next to me, was a young woman by the name of Rumana. We had a brief introduction and then the class began. Pru started the process of pairing the students up. Rumana was selected to be the Viewer for my target I had set up, while I was to *monitor* her progress but at no time were we allowed to divulge anything about our targets.

Rumana went first. I read out the target coordinates which she duly took, and started the remote viewing. Without a word from me, she began drawing the hill in uncanny accuracy, as well the nearby road. I said nothing as I watched her struggle till she could no longer come up with any more data.

As always with trainee viewers, we often think we have completely missed our targets prior to seeing our feedback. It was no different with Rumana.

It was now time for us to reveal the feedback. I finally showed Rumana the photo, and commended the work she did on her amazing sketch and description of the target. She marvelled at her work, and we wrapped up the session. I must say I was pretty impressed and just could not believe the sketch Rumana had just drawn.

After a few more comments by Pru on the TDS remote viewing structure, we switched roles and it was now my turn to remote view Rumana's target. Rumana showed Pru her target choice, which we all had to do to ensure the targets we had picked would be suitable for others to view. Pru gave her the go ahead that it was fine and we were off.

I had no idea what I was about to let myself in for.

The session started as normal, but for some strange reason, halfway through, my body started getting warmer and warmer. At first I thought it was just nerves, but there was something else at play, or so I thought.

I was stuck.

I could not make sense of what I was getting. I was expecting buildings or something physical that I could describe but all I kept getting was intense feelings....of *something*. What the hell was it? I looked up at my monitor, Rumana; she didn't even look me in the eye, she was giving absolutely nothing away...nothing, nada, zilch.

By this time my hands were getting warmer, my body felt like it was about to explode, not with pain, but with a warmth I had never felt before. Now my breathing started to get heavier, I noticed Pru making her way through the class, leaning over each desk and pairs of students, by the time she reached my desk, I said, "Pru I don't know what I've got here, but I'm having a hard time putting it into words, and whatever it is, it's affecting my body". Pru said nothing, apart from assuring Rumana the target was fine. It was very frustrating indeed. The whole thing reminded me of that famous scene in the Steven Spielberg movie *Close Encounters of the Third Kind* where Richard Dreyfuss struggles desperately to make sense of the psychic impressions imprinted in his mind of what turned out eventually to be Devils Tower in Wyoming.

Yet this was real. This was no Hollywood movie. I could *feel* the target but had no way of interpreting those feelings or maybe…I was in denial?

Towards the end, I had no choice but to declare, as best I could, what I was feeling and experiencing from the session. I remember thinking to myself, "God, I'm going to look like a fool when I see the feedback", even worse, we had been told we will have to stand in front of the class and read out our OWN summaries of the target. Talk about ultimate humiliation!

The more I tried to fight the *one word* I felt best described my target the warmer I got and the more embarrassed I felt.

I thought to myself," I can't write that". It would make no sense at all. In the end it was all too much and I wrote just one word as large as possible which filled out the whole A4 paper. I was done.

I was probably one of the last in the class to finish their sessions. Pru instructed the monitors to reveal their respective feedbacks to the remote viewers.

Rumana finally revealed what the target was and I was immediately stunned:

"Describe the cure for Cancer"

Amongst some of the sketches I had drawn were round objects which looked like blood cells or cells of some kind indeed I even wrote *blood* on them, the word *light* popped up in several places and then there was that last word I had written so large on the final page.

I sat quietly as I awaited my turn to be called up in front of the whole class and go through my session, step by step. I got up and made my way to the front of the class. I looked up...all eyes were on me.

I told them what the target was and what I had drawn, which seemed to generate a lot of chatter at the time, and then I nervously revealed the final page and the final word which drew gasps and some applause, if I remember correctly. That word was simply:

"LOVE"

The word I struggled for ages, to dare write down, and the word that brought warmth I had never truly felt until that moment and yearn to feel in its intensity again, a word filled with so much light and possibilities. Could *this* really be the cure for cancer? No one seemed to think otherwise that day, especially Rumana herself. She simply shrugged her shoulders as if she EXPECTED that 'word' to be the answer. What I *didn't* know prior to doing the viewing, was that Rumana was a practicing *healer* and according to her, ALL healing was based on *love* and is what she herself used on her clients. It is important to point out that these are simply training targets and not uncommon for monitors to know what the target is although it still violates basic protocol, however, having said that, for this particular target I would never in a million years have guessed I would ever have been given such a target. I was expecting a more grounded target, something I could evaluate and verify which makes this particular target and the data that came out of the session and how it made me *"feel"* at the time, quite remarkable at least from my point of view.

Fourteen years on, Rumana now runs a respected healing naturopath practice here in the U.K. Her vision is to encourage individuals to take a pro-active and multi-disciplined approach to achieving the very best of health, using natural medicine where possible.

I finally made my way home that evening after class. It was a memorable day and I am still in touch with a few of those students, some I'm sure, will read this one day and remember fondly what we achieved. I was a changed man after that session. Not in any obvious way but *something* inside me had changed or had been 'awakened'. I sometimes get *that* feeling of love from time to time often when around loved ones or through prayer or meditation but rarely as powerful as it was on that cold November Saturday.

To this day the cure for cancer target remains one of the most memorable remote viewing sessions I have ever done.[6]

Eventually, I was invited to join the TDS online training program for six months and if I did well, I was to join them full time as a professional viewer, something I was looking forward to in the long term. However this was not to be. Within a month, TDS was mysteriously shutdown by Pru. She retired completely from all remote viewing activities under circumstances still not entirely explained today. I spoke to several former members to find out what happened but it appears there was just too much pressure on the company from very *sinister* individuals whom it would seem were not entirely happy with TDS's commercial activities within the public domain as a private company since remote viewing had been declassified.

One thing was clear from the various individuals I spoke to; they were definitely under surveillance by certain intelligence agencies. Tales of electronic surveillance systems or 'bugs' being discovered at members homes and on TDS premises, as well as white vans parked outside with covert listening devices were the order of the day. It's impossible to verify most of these claims.

At the height of their success, Pru and TDS claimed to provide RV services to certain companies on Wall Street, advised on high profile corporate mergers, and even the serving *chairman of the Federal Reserve Board* at that time took an interest in what the company was doing.[7]

One of those mergers I happen to know for a fact did take place. I am not at liberty to discuss the company names, only that TDS was approached by a major hedge fund firm to assess a proposed merger bid which in the end turned out to be a major success, in fact one of the few successful mergers during the dot.com boom era.

The hedge fund company in question who hired TDS's services *made a fortune* on the predicted outcome of their investment.

This proves to me that there is indeed a market for RV in the corporate world but due to the stigma attached to all things "psychic", no hedge fund firm is ready to admit to hiring remote viewers to predict the outcome of mergers or stock market trends. However Joe McMoneagle believes more corporations are utilizing remote viewing behind the scenes:

*"The bottom line is, a company could still honestly develop an advantage over another by simply targeting **the future**. I honestly believe there are*

corporations in other countries who have already begun to develop their own remote viewing departments and capabilities. It is not a band-wagon which will remain in one place. Now is the time to get on."[8]

Eventually, after numerous independent correspondence and discussions with some of the key TDS players I do believe there was an element of truth to some of these claims even though they remain for the most part still cloaked in secrecy and speculation. Hopefully former members and perhaps maybe even Pru herself will one day come forward and shed more light on what really happened.

Over the years, I continued to practice as best I could, alone at first, just using a small private target pool I had created consisting of locations around the world and a few historic events which were written on paper and sealed in brown envelopes.

I simply picked an envelope from the pile and would try to remote view the contents of the envelope I had selected. It was fun for a while; however I craved working with a group of serious dedicated remote viewers rather than just on my own. Having a small pool of targets didn't help either. I needed external validation from others rather than just working on my own. I wanted something similar to what I had experienced during training and collaborate with like-minded individuals. I needed to broaden my skills and get the viewpoints of fellow viewers such as myself, still fresh out of training and rough round the edges, as well as engage in debate and the sharing of knowledge with more experienced viewers.

Back in those days, accurate and reliable information was hard to come by unless you were one of the lucky ones to take advanced training with any of the ex-military viewers. However I wanted more, I wanted interaction and stimulation to keep my interest in RV on a high.

I eventually ended up setting up my own private practice RV group forum called **SiriusRV**. I managed to get on board a few former TDS viewers with the aim of doing weekly targets, remote viewing projects, sharing sessions and perform group analysis. There were five of us initially, myself, Jon, Jeane, Bill and Roma. Four other viewers (non TDS) eventually joined the group including Glyn, Liz, Kristen, Rob, and Damien.

Another enthusiastic viewer who joined my group was a guy called Darryl Smith. Daz, as he likes to be called, was a CRV trained remote viewer I came across in one of the online remote viewing forums and who lived in Bath, here in the U.K. Today, Daz runs one of the largest remote viewing online sites in the world and is also the owner and editor of the community's largest remote viewing magazine called *Eight Martinis*. He currently works as a full time professional remote viewer, offering his services to police departments in various countries, working on TV documentaries, Radio Talk shows, live online demonstrations as well as publishing two books on remote viewing and is widely regarded as one of the best CRV professionals around today.

Together, as a group, we worked targets for just over four years until 2007, occasionally changing the name of the core group till we ended up with our final group called *The Aurora Group*.

The Aurora Group was a bold attempt by a handful of dedicated viewers to provide remote viewing services to the public as well as continue our own development as a practice and research group.

Eventually it disbanded after a split in opinion in where the group was heading while some viewers went off and did their own thing.

Some of the work we did was among the best I've ever seen from a group of remote viewers. In some ways we were a victim of our own success perhaps. Some members wanted to focus on providing ARV (Associative Remote Viewing) services or what we called *'outcome'* work (sports prediction service) while some wanted to provide services such as looking for missing people or solving crimes etc.

Since those days, I have continued to work on and off with individuals who ask for my skills and today I mainly use RV for practice, fun or exploratory projects. One recent project I was asked to take part in was to help search for the missing Malaysian Airline MH370.

This book will highlight some of the work I have produced either as myself or in collaboration with other viewers. It is hoped the reader will enjoy these sessions and accept them for what they are; examples of remote viewing sessions done under strict blind protocols and at various levels of expertise from beginner level to the more advanced stages and finally to the 'final frontiers' and beyond. Remote Viewing targets which, for the most part, will remain unverified, until we have sufficient feedback – hopefully within the reader's lifetime.

These examples will also highlight some of the pitfalls to avoid when it comes to remote viewing targets of an unknown and unverifiable nature and hopefully benefit students of RV whenever they encounter similar projects.

Remote Viewing Examples

Here are a couple of RV examples of validated targets (targets with known and **verifiable feedback**) that I have done for others over the years.

The following target was sent to an online Remote Viewing practice group I was a member of including several other viewers. No one was given any information other than a target reference number. The target was done completely blind by myself and alone. Apart from naming the target event itself, I also honed in on something totally *unexpected.*

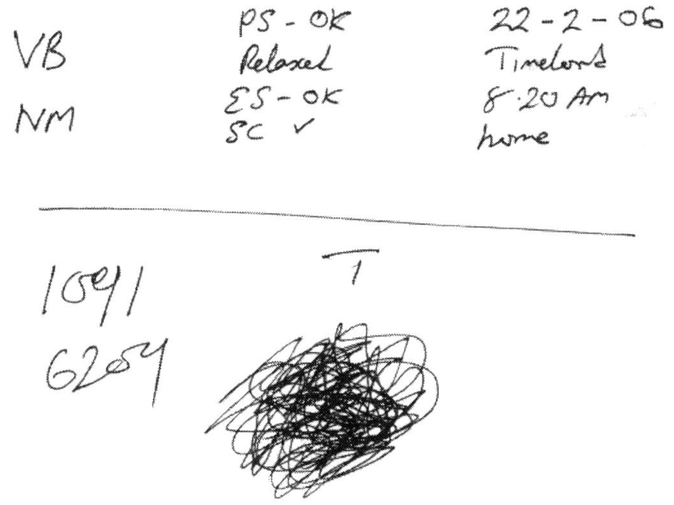

VB
NM

PS - OK
Relaxed
ES - OK
SC ✓

22 - 2 - 06
Timelord
8:20 Am
home

1091
6205

1

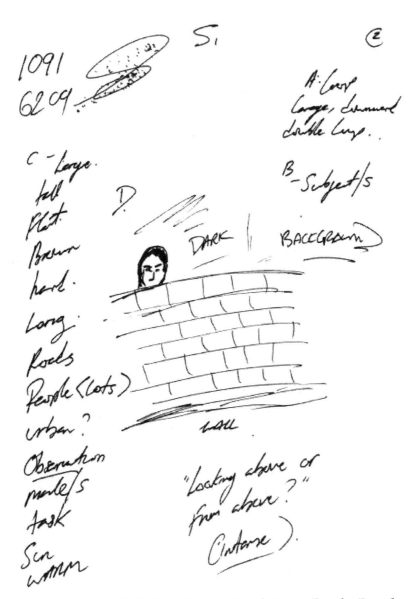

Transcript – Large, Tall, Flat, Brown, Hard, Long, Roads, **People (lots),** urban? Observation, **Male/s,** Task, Sun, Warm, **WALL,** Background, "Looking above or from above?" **(Intense)**

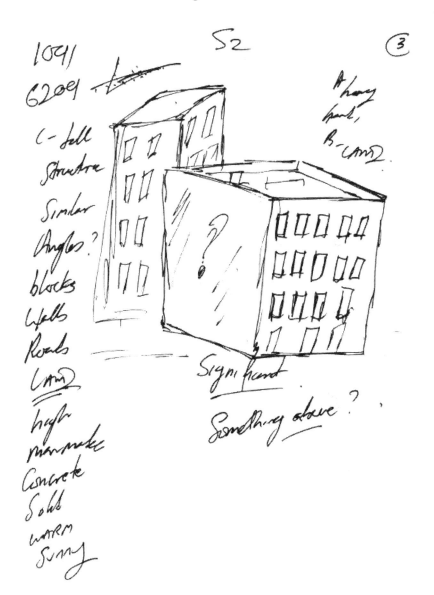

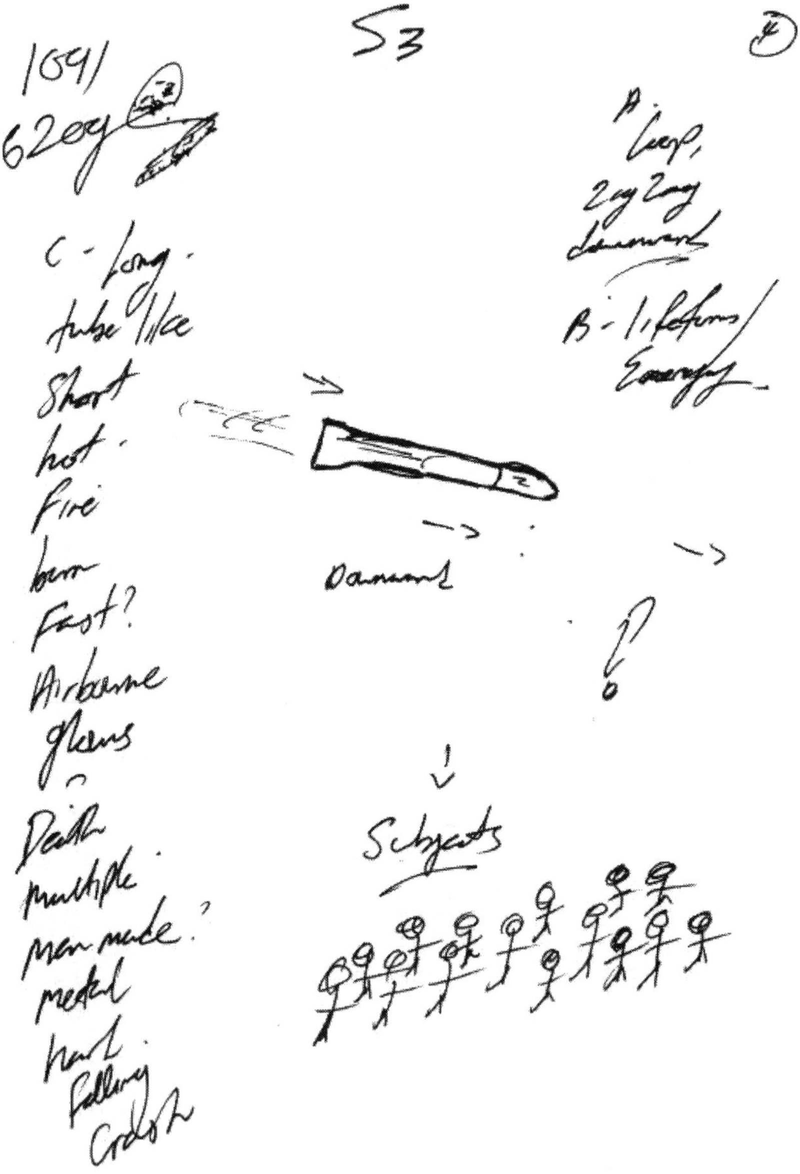

1091
62 org

S3

C - long.
tube like
Short
hot.
fire
burn
Fast?
Airborne
gleans

Death
multiple.
man made?
medal
hard
falling
Crash

A "leep,
2 org 2 org
Downward

B - life forms /
Energy

Downward

?

Subjects

Transcript OC - [S1] Male/s, lifeforms, hidden, hide, out of sight,
Protection, hair, dark, sweaty, tense, white, green, black, barrier, crouch
[S2] Tall, hard, building, squad?, windows –many, on top? Monument,
history [S3] Dart, fall, craft, metal, small, missile, tube, fast, people, Uh Oh!
Bullet?

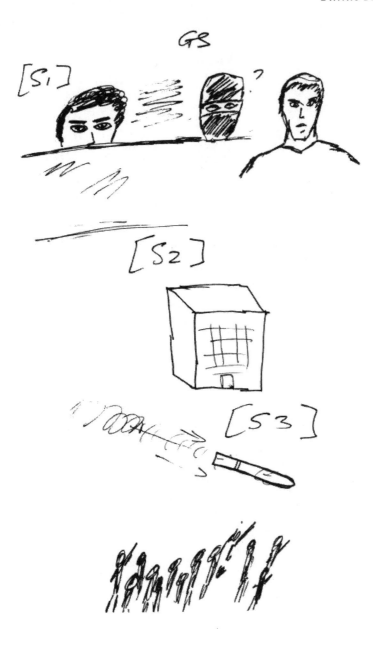

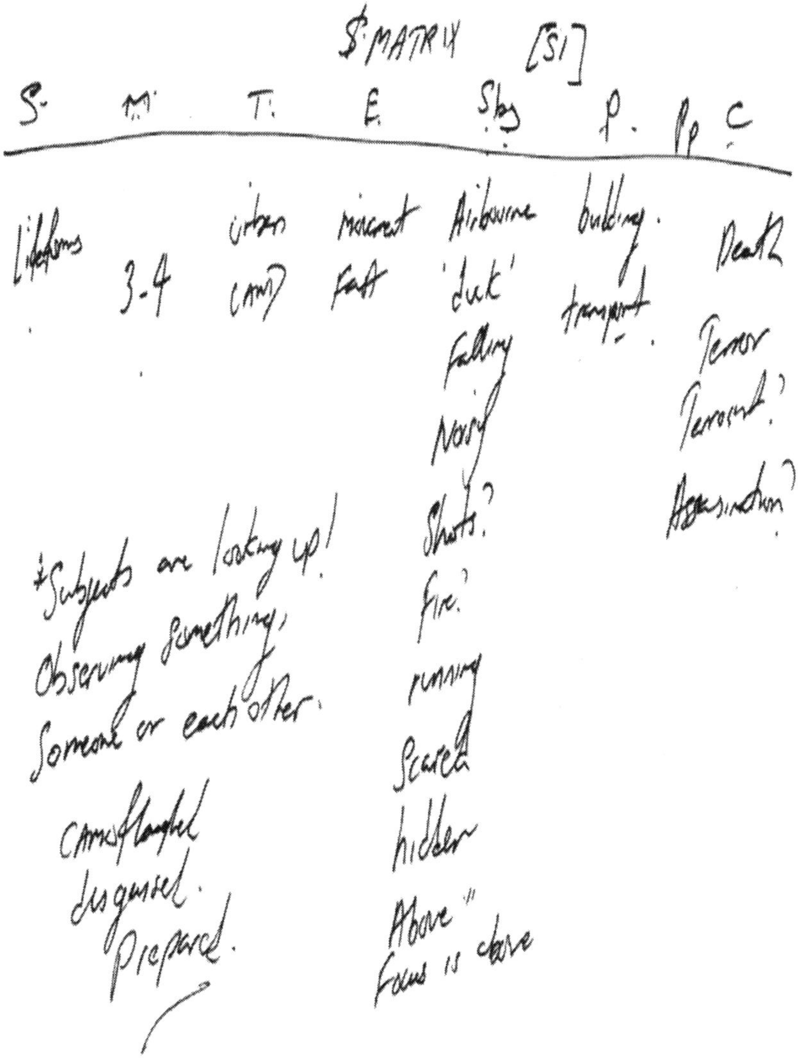

$\$ MATRIX \quad [SI]$

S.　M.　T.　E.　Sby　P.　Pp　C

Lifeforms

3-4　urban　innocent　Airborne　building.　Death
　　　　camp　fast　'duck'　transport.　Terror
　　　　　　　　falling　　　　　Terrorist?
　　　　　　　　Noisy
　　　　　　　　Shots?　　　　　Assassination?
　　　　　　　　fire?
*Subjects are looking up!　running
Observing something,　scared
Someone or each other.　hidden
Camouflaged　Above"
disguised.　Focus is above
Prepared.

Subjects are looking up! Observing something, someone or each other.
Camouflaged, disguised, <u>Prepared.</u> Airborne, duck, falling, noisy, **Shots –
Fire, running scared, above,** Focus is above, **Building, Transport, Death,
Terror, Terrorist?, Assassination?**

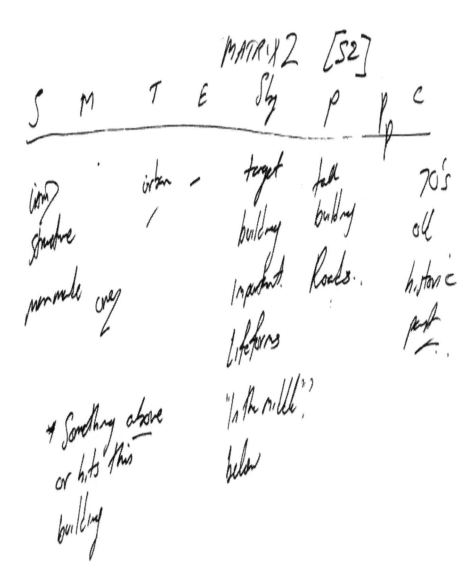

Something <u>above</u> or hits this building, urban, Target, Building, important, lifeforms, *"In The Middle?"*, below, tall, building, Roads, 70's (1970's), old, Historic, <u>Past</u>.

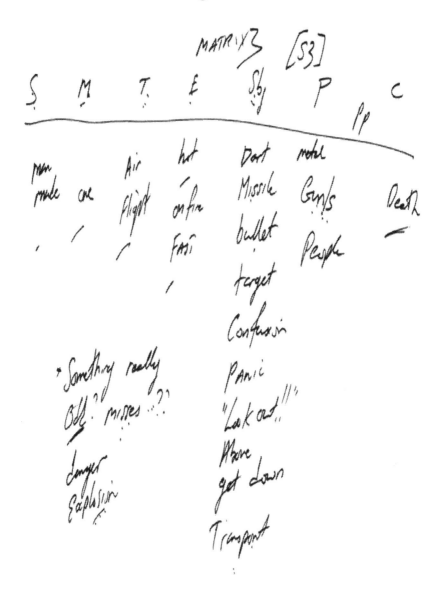

Man Made, Something really Odd? Misses? Danger, explosion, air, flight, hot, on fire, fast, Dart, missile, bullet, target, confusion, panic, "Look Out!!", above, get down, Transport, Metal, Gun/s, People...DEATH

*focus on what tasker needs
to know.
Target site is one of terror
and panic. Subjects are afraid
and running helter skelter.
"Something" is coming down on
them. Not pleasant... Death!
Feels like a terror attack
but I suspect this has already
happened. Sense a very strong
"military" Connection, covert perhaps
as subjects appear to be crouching
or hidding while others appear
to be out in the open.
More than one subject is
armed. These armed individuals
are all at target site but
at opposite Ends?*

*Focus on what tasker needs to *know* – Target site is one of terror and panic. Subjects (people) are afraid and running helter skelter. "*Something*" is coming down on them. Not Pleasant...**Death!** Feels like a terror attack but I suspect this has already happened. Sense a very strong "*military*" connection, "*covert*" perhaps as subjects appear to be crouching or hiding while others appear to be out in the open. More than one subject is *armed*. These armed individuals are all at the target site but at **opposite ends?**

Continued. →

Looks like a Street battle, Chaos & fighting with Civilians Caught up. Whatever this is, it is **BIG**!!

[S₁] shows some men hiding behind a wall? Could be symbolic AOL The Alamo.
— Also sense transport as well Something is moving ....

[S₂] Not sure what this building has to do with the target but is obviously important and is in the middle of the battle scene

Transcript – Continued – Looks like a street battle, chaos and fighting with civilians caught up. Whatever this is, it is **BIG!!** **[S1] shows some men hiding behind a <u>wall?</u>** Could be symbolic AOL the Alamo. Also sense **transport** – *something is moving* ... **[S2]** Not sure what this building has to do with the target but is obviously important and is in the middle of the battle scene

Continued -

[S3] tube or bullet like device is on fire and coming down. People are taking evasive action and running for their lives.

I suspect this is connected with the [S1] individuals hidden BUT why is everyone looking above??? weird.

Transcript - Continued – **[S3]** Tube or bullet-like device is on fire and coming down. People are taking evasive action and running for their lives. I suspect this is connected with the **[S1]** individuals hidden <u>BUT</u> why is everyone looking above??? weird.

*focus on DEATH at target site
and the outcome

Two very strong AOL's spring
to mind. 1) Catastrophic terror
attack and planned assasination
of JFK.
The impact or 'feelings' I'm
getting are on par with 911 attacks
which brought the whole world
to focus on this one activity.
Whatever it is, it was truly
shocking. The full story has not
been told. Secrecy is involved here.

*Focus on <u>DEATH</u> at target site and the outcome – TWO very strong AOLs spring to mind 1) Catastrophic terror attack and planned assasination of **JFK**. The impact or 'feelings' I'm getting are on par with 911 attacks which brought the whole world to focus on this one activity. Whatever it *(the target)* is, it was trully shocking. The full story has not been told. Secrecy is involved here.

Summary

wow! Cant wait to see feedback
on this one. Even if I am not
on target the emotions & feeling
of subject at the target
cannot be ignored.
Something is being witnessed that
will literally or more than
likely already has changed the
course of history.
This is either a terrorist attack
or assassination of JFK.

End

Transcript – Summary

"Wow can't wait to see feedback on this one. Even if I'm not on target, the emotions and feelings of subjects (people) at the target **cannot** be ignored. Something is being witnessed, or more than likely, already has changed the course of history. This is either a terrorist attack or assassination of **JFK**" - END

Target:

1091 - 6209

The Grassy Knoll - Dallas on November 23, 1963, 12,28

Tasking:

Move to the optimum position and describe the place known as the 'grassy knoll', describe any life forms at this place, describe the unfolding event.

Feedback:

Minutes after the shooting, Dallas Times Herald photographer William Allen ran from the newspaper building to Dealey Plaza and caught this view of bystanders milling around Dallas Police officer Clyde Haygood's motorcycle at the foot of the grassy knoll. The names of most of these people are unknown. An unidentified officer peered over the picket fence at a spot where some witnesses thought a shot originated.

Shot sequencing and origins

There was a clear consensus among the witnesses as to the number of shots: over 90% thought there were three or fewer shots. More witnesses thought the final two shots were bunched together than thought the shots were evenly spaced, or that the first two were bunched.

Of the witnesses who gave some testimony as to the source of the shots, 35 thought the shots came from the direction of the Grassy Knoll, 56 thought the shots came from the direction of the School Book Depository, eight thought the shots came from an entirely different location (including two who thought the shots came from inside the limo). Only five witnesses thought the shots came from two different locations.

Here is another typical example of remote viewing. This time, using a combination of *two methods*. The first method, the Eye Blink Procedure EBP as created by Joe E. Slate PhD, and the TDS method I was originally trained in.

This particular target was set up by Daz Smith and sent to me as part of a public experiment to test Joe Slate's new EBP/RV method as published in his book, *Beyond Reincarnation*. I had recently raised the topic of exploring the use of hypnosis for remote viewing purposes on the TKR Remote Viewing online forum. I announced I would test Slate's method and report back to members and let them know my findings. Daz kindly volunteered to send me a target via email, one with **100% verifiable feedback** so we could assess the accuracy of the viewing overall.

Once again, I remote viewed the target completely alone. No other information was given other than the following numbers below which is purely used for reference purposes only. The target could have been anything, any place, about anyone at any time.

7764 - 5521

ERV

NMI

BLIND

ES -ok
PS -ok

Time

13:20

19-4-06

---

* A Short ERV excursion to the target 7764-5521 has already been completed.
This is a further breakdown of the impression picked up from that initial excursion.

7764
5521

Transcript- "A Short ERV excursion to the target 7764-5521 has already been completed. This is a further breakdown of the impressions picked up from that initial excursion"

[Sketch shows **water way** and **a bridge** as viewed from above] land, water, underneath me is water, solid structure, above water? Embankments?

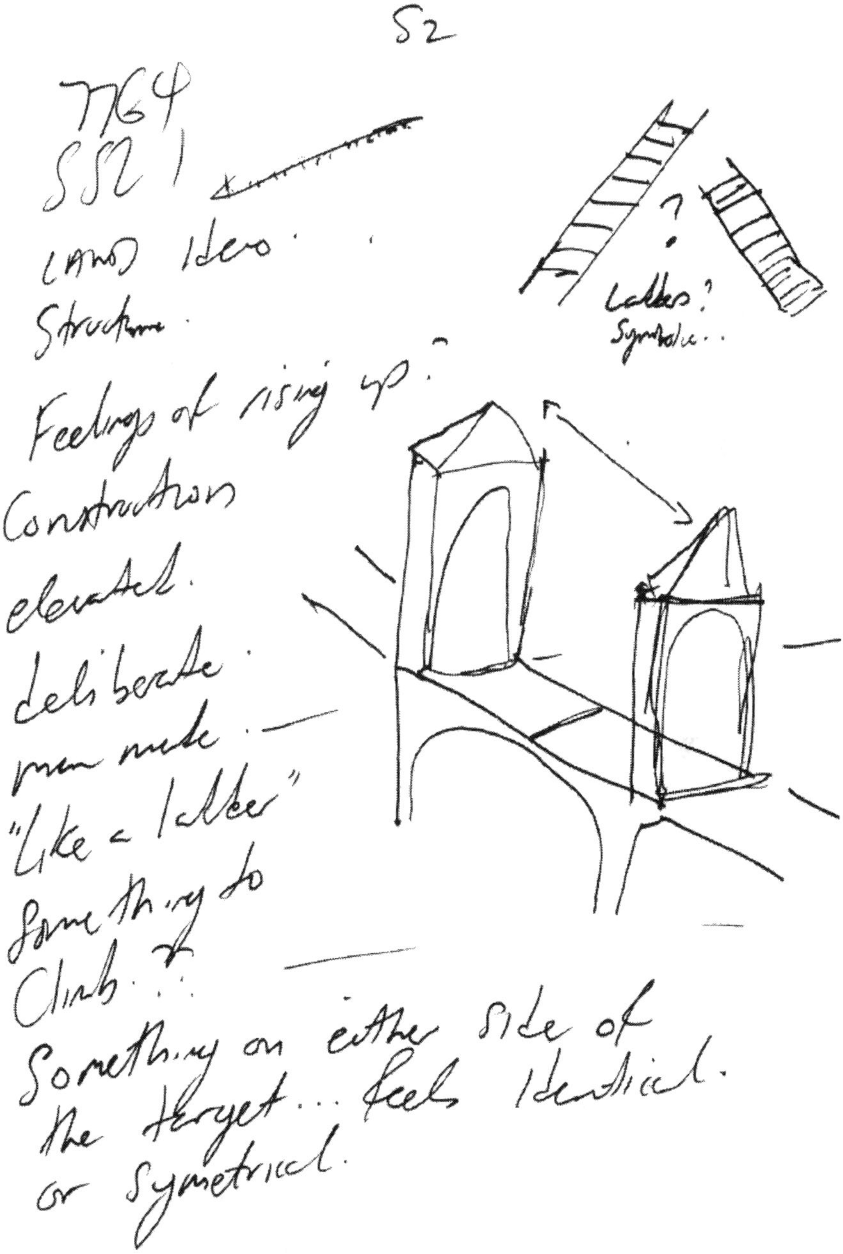

S2

7764
SS2

(LAND) Idea.

Structure.

Feelings of rising up.

Construction

elevated.

deliberate

man made. ——

"Like a ladder"

Something to

Climb. ?.

Ladder?
Symbolic...

Something on either side of
the target... feels Identical.
or symetrical.

Summary.

[Handwritten note:]

Target wasn't very clear in my mind but i did sense man made 'physical' structure located nearby water also connected to (LAND).

The feeling of Climbing or rising represented by what looked like a ladder or Flat tall device was Strong.

Also there was water beneath me at target Site.

If i didn't know any better i would say it was a bridge of some kind but not just any old bridge.

"Transcript – Target wasn't very clear in my mind but I did sense a man-made 'physical' structure located nearby **water** also connected to <u>land</u>. The feeling of climbing or rising represented by what looked like a ladder or flat tall device was strong. Also there was **water** beneath me at target site. If I didn't know any better I would say it was **a bridge of some kind** but not just any **old bridge**."

86

Summary Continued ..

There was a large AOL of
what looked like London Bridge
as a saw something being raised
on both sides in a mechanical
method. Plus the strong feeling
that water was beneath me
was also very high.

Will End Session here.

End [signature]

"There was a large AOL (Analytical Overlay) of what looked *like* **London Bridge** as I saw something raised on both sides in a mechanical method, plus the strong feeling that **water** was beneath me was also very high. Will end session here. End."

The feedback

7764-5521

Brooklyn Bridge, New York, Time of photograph

Tasking:

Move to the optimum position/location and describe the focus of the photograph at the time of the photograph.

As you can see the session was a success and highlights the many techniques and methods one can use to perform remote viewing. I tend to use a combination of the Extended Remote Viewing/EPB method for a more *immersive* experience with the target even though it is harder to maintain focus with this particular method. The second method I use on a regular basis is the standard TDS method as demonstrated with the JFK/Grassy Knoll session.

The most important thing the reader should bear in mind regardless of whatever method you use, is the appropriate blind protocol that **must** be adhered to and the availability of feedback to prove and measure the accuracy of the person doing the remote viewing.

CHAPTER 6

Beyond Remote Viewing: Exploratory and Speculative Examples of Remote Viewing

- *"Two possibilities exits … Either we are alone in the universe or we are not. Both are equally terrifying."* - **Arthur C Clarke**

It has been said by some experts of RV and with good cause I must add, that Remote Viewing without any real feedback to analyse and assess the accuracy of the remote viewing done - is a waste of time. This is essentially true, so one might wonder why I decided to write a book primarily about stuff that we do not have full feedback on.

The answer to this question is quite simple from my perspective, which is, I do this purely for research, exploration and basic human curiosity. Also the targets, for the most part, have been carefully selected, based on the amount of *confirmed* and *verifiable* feedback we do have which will be revealed to the viewer at the end of each project. Finally, while not content to just view objects and known locations to prove the reality of PSI, I am forever looking to learn new things, test the waters, explore the limits and shed some light on some of our biggest mysteries as a species and God knows there are plenty of things we still do not know about ourselves and the fundamental questions of our time. What is consciousness? Where does consciousness originate from? Why are we here? Where are we going?

Are we alone……?

Remote Viewing UFOS and The Visitors

That last question has been on my mind since childhood. I can still recall picking out my very first library book in Stockwell, London, It was a UFO book which fascinating me but at the same time caused immense frustration because I couldn't understand or read all the words. Science had no real answer back in those days for a 7 year old kid concerning the UFO phenomenon and sadly some *forty plus* years later, we are no closer to resolving the mystery once and for all. However, as our knowledge about the universe grows, we are getting much closer than ever before in trying to unravel the questions poised about our place in the cosmos. Our satellites have looked deeper into space, showing us the beginnings of the universe, and potential evidence to back up the big bang theory. We now know roughly, just how old the universe is, we are discovering more galaxies, more stars, more planets on a daily basis.

It will only be a matter of time till we finally find a way to venture beyond our planet once again and step foot on another world. While our space programs seem to have stopped at putting man on the moon it is inevitable we will return to the stars in a big way, hopefully within the next 50 – 150 years.

Based on this assumption, I decided to see what remote viewing could do in order to at least assist in our understanding of what really lies *out there*, until such time as we are able to verify any findings remote viewing will produce.

As a result, this project can be viewed as an elaborate experiment in feedback in relation to some of the questions raised in the data you are about to read in this book. How long will it take for some of the feedback to be verified? Hopefully not long at all, in fact *some* of the data has already been verified and I have no doubt we will have concrete answers within the next 50 to 80 years.

In the meantime, it is hoped those blessed with an open mind, and similar curiosity as my own, but with a much superior degree of scientific knowledge, will take on board some of the fascinating information presented here for the first time, derived via *Remote viewing.*

I do realise we may never get feedback during our lifetime but once again, my hope is future generations will be able to read the findings of this book and perhaps help those generations gain further insight in their own understanding of how the mind works and eventually prove we were at the very least, on *the right path.*

I also hope those of you reading this - especially those within the scientific community- take a leap of faith and simply accept the data in the book for what it is, and allow it to be used as just another form of *normal* intelligence gathering, to support existing theories and ultimately aid in providing clues and answers where none are currently available or deliberately being withheld from the general public.

Ingo Swann and the Jupiter Probe:

One of the earliest examples of using remote viewing for space exploratory purposes was done by Ingo Swann back in 1973.

Swann proposed a study to Stanford Research Institute scientists, during ongoing research into remote viewing, using a specific protocol he developed called SCANATE (Scanning by Coordinates). The idea behind SCANATE was based on Swan's belief he could describe any location anywhere using only that locations geographic coordinates. SCANATE turned out to be a success for SRI and agencies such as the CIA, but Ingo wanted to push the limits of Remote Viewing and see just how far a remote viewer could reach.

He came up with the idea of exploring the planet Jupiter prior to NASA's Pioneer 10 rendezvous with the gas giant.

At first the idea was resisted, for the resulting descriptions would be impossible to verify and outside standard RV protocol. However, on the evening of 27th April 1973, SRI researchers Russell Targ and Hal Puthoff recorded Swann's remote viewing session of the planet Jupiter *prior* to the Voyager space probe's visit there in 1979.

"Swann asked for 30 minutes of silence. According to Swann, his ability to see Jupiter took about three and a half minutes. In the session he made several reports on the physical features of Jupiter, such as its surface, atmosphere and weather. Swann's statement that *Jupiter had planetary rings, like Saturn,* was controversial at the time. The 1979 Voyager 1 probe later confirmed the existence of the rings."[9]

Skeptics however continue to debate the accuracy of some of Swann's results but there does not seem to be any disputing the fact he *did* describe *multiple* things (not just the famous rings) about Jupiter that was not 100% known at the time by scientist or fully verified.

Unlike the famous Swann experiment, the sessions presented here were all done without the remote viewer even knowing what the target will be and the remote viewers given absolutely no information up front making the data all the more remarkable as we shall see.

Another famous case and use of RV, to explore remote locations outside of our verifiable abilities at the time, involved America's top remote viewer and former military psychic spy,

Joseph W McMoneagle.

Joe was given a series of blind targets by his RV monitor, Skip Atwater. The date was 22nd May 1984. During a routine training session held at the Monroe Institute in Virginia USA, Joe described **eight** different *coordinate locations* under double blind protocols. The targets were once again provided by the same team involved in Ingo Swann's Jupiter fly-by session at SRI involving Hal Puthoff. The targets were initially passed to Robert Monroe, who ran the Monroe Institute at the time, to see what a skilled remote viewer would come up with.

The targets were prepared and the session commenced with Skip monitoring Joe as he began to describe the cryptic locations he was given. Remember, neither of these men knew what the targets were or who the client or taskers were. What followed was an astonishing tale of a lost civilization, megalithic structures of various shapes but mainly pyramids which seemed to dwarf the largest known pyramids found here on earth. Joe had no idea what or where he was viewing but continued describing *tall* humanoid beings who seemed to be have been involved in some cataclysmic event.

Once Joe had finished his remote viewing he was eventually given feedback by Skip. The target was:

"The Planet Mars, One million years BC"

The remaining targets included actual original NASA images taken by the Viking 1 Orbiter in 1976, which at the time, and still do to this day, generated immense speculation as to what the structures were.

Some of the targets were of a specific region known as Cydonia which appears to be littered with many structures, which at the time, appeared to be artificial including the infamous *Face on Mars*.

For a full report, as well as actual detailed remote viewing session sketches drawn by Joe, I recommend you read his excellent book, *MIND TREK – Exploring Consciousness, Time and Space through Remote Viewing.*

As amazing as these examples of speculative viewing are, we cannot know for certain how accurate the data produced is until we have feedback to match that data. But what the data does support is the need to investigate these areas on Mars. Brave committed scientists might be able to look beyond the way in which this remote viewing data was produced, or its use as just another intelligence gathering tool, and focus more on how much of the data generated actually supports what we DO know for sure about Mars and the Cydonia region already. This region has generated controversy, intrigue, mystery and debate ever since the first Viking images were sent back to earth, and to a stunned NASA.

Today, Joe believes we will one day – within this century - establish that there once was life on Mars which existed over a million years ago, along with an unknown race of beings no longer there. Indeed Joe goes further to add the human race may in fact be descendants of those early 'Martians'.

Will Joe be proven right? We may never know, but for now however, I am confident we will eventually get the feedback which will either validate or invalidate the data once we finally step foot on the dusty surface of Mars and begin to explore its surface in depth. In the meantime it remains a very fascinating piece of the puzzle with regards to whether or not we are alone in the universe.

CHAPTER 7

Fatima and the Miracle of the Sun
UFO Case #1

"As a multiplicity of creatures exist on earth, so there could be other beings, also intelligent, created by God. This does not contrast with our faith because we cannot put limits on the creative freedom of God. To say it with Saint Francis, if we consider earthly creatures as "brother" and "sister," why cannot we also speak of an 'extraterrestrial brother?' It would therefore be a part of creation."

- ***Father José Gabriel Funes***,
  Director of the Vatican Observatory, 2008

You could almost picture the scene in your mind, thousands of devotees, all gazing up to the heavens on a cloudy dull and wet morning. The multitudes gathered waiting, expecting, praying and with nothing to go on other than their deep rooted faith and on the backdrop of a most devastating World War consuming most of Europe.

The location: Fatima , Portugal Cova de Iris...

Over 60,000 estimated witnesses made their way to the muddy fields of Cova De Iria, near Fatima after a series of predictions and the testimony of three local children. Over a period of 6 months, the children repeatedly claimed to have been visited by a *Lady of Light,* dressed in *strange clothing,* whose lips did not move, yet could be heard speaking directly to them according to the reports. The mysterious lady also allegedly revealed a series of 'secrets and warnings.' The third and most controversial of those secrets has been the subject of rumours, speculation and numerous conspiracy theories for decades.

The contents of those 'secrets', sadly, are outside the scope of this presentation, although, I will attempt to raise certain questions by the end of this report, for reasons I hope will be clear to the reader based on the evidence at hand.

However, what we do know for a fact, and can be corroborated by the numerous eyewitness testimonies, was the mass meeting of thousands of people at this one particular location with the sole ambition of witnessing a promised miracle. It appears they were not disappointed.

Lucia Santos (age 10, pictured in the middle) and her two cousins: Francisco (age 9) and Jacinta Marto (age 7) holding their rosaries. Fatima, Portugal.

The 13th Day

The true events leading up to what is now known as The *Miracle of the* Sun began with the visions of three local children. Between May 13th to October 13th 1917, **Lúcia Santos** and her cousins **Jacinta** and **Francisco Marto** reported visions of a *luminous lady*, believed to be the Virgin Mary, in the Cova da Iria fields outside the hamlet of Aljustrel, near Fátima, Portugal. *[There are new reports of a 'fourth seer' who saw visions of the Virgin Mary in the same vicinity and around the same time – Carolina Carreira.]* 10

The children claimed the visitations took place on the *13th day of each month at approximately noon, for six straight months*11. The one exception apparently was August; the children were kidnapped by a local administrator. That month they did not report a vision of the Lady until after they were released from jail, some days later.

Here is what Lucia Santos, the primary seer, had to say about that first initial encounter with *'The Lady'* along with her cousins:

"We saw a Lady over an oak tree, dressed all in white, more brilliantly than the Sun, sparkling with a light more clear and intense than a crystal glass full of water shot through by the most ardent rays of the Sun. We stopped, surprised by the Apparition. We were so close that we were within the light that enclosed her, or which she scattered, perhaps a meter and a half away, more or less."[12]

'The Lady' advised the children to return to the same location every month on the 13th day. She allegedly revealed a series of three *secrets* to Lucia. The mysterious lady then promised she would deliver a miracle to the church faithful on the 13th day of October. Word spread like wildfire and the children became overnight sensations, drawing thousands of believers to each apparitional event and the Vatican church, into their lives - forever.

So what really happened on that final promised visit from this mysterious 'lady of light'? Reports vary, yet remain remarkably consistent according to the documentation of that era, but most historians concede, some form of meteorological activity did in fact take place. Amongst some of the actual witness statements are observations such as: The *Sun* appearing to *'move'* or *fall* towards the earth, spinning, rotating and giving off *'heat'*. Various colours were reported in the sky, and strange hair like substances falling from above.

Canon Formigao – *"The sun at its zenith spun dizzyingly upon itself like the most beautiful wheel of fireworks that one could imagine"*

Maria Celeste da Camara Vasconcelos – *"The Sun began to spin in circles of every colour like a wheel of fireworks"*

Maria Teresa de Chainca – *(who was 30 meters from the site of the Apparitions) "The sky was covered with clouds and it was raining heavily. We could not see the Sun. Then suddenly at noon, the clouds parted and the Sun emerged as if trembling, appearing to descend, and **giving off great heat"**[13]*

Pinto Coelho – *"Separating itself from the Sun [The Object] approached the Earth, **and radiated strong heat"**[14]*

Luis de Andrade e Silver - Testified on **December 30, 1917:**

*"Someone at my side called my attention to the Sun, and I noted something in its behaviour that until this day I had never seen. The orb of the Sun, spun around on the imaginary axis, and at that moment appeared to descend in the atmosphere, towards Earth, accompanied at times by an **extraordinary brilliance and a very intense heat.**"[15]*

Higino Fari – *"Through the aperture of the parted cloud, we saw the Sun shining, spinning like a wheel of fire"*

Maria Teresa, de Chainca – *"Afterwards, the Sun began spinning like a wheel of fire during popular celebrations"*

101

Avelino de Almeida – *"To the impressionable eyes of the crowd...the Sun trembled, the Sun had never seen sudden movements, outside of all cosmic laws - the Sun "danced", according to the typical expression of the country folk".* In his article published by Illustracao Portuguesa, de Almeida described what he himself actually witnessed that day, *"What did I see? The Sun – a disk of dull silver in full zenith appeared and began dancing in a violent and convulsive dance"*[16]

These are just a small sample of literally thousands of similar reports, some of which were published in the Portuguese press after the miracle. As one can clearly see, in a majority of these reports, the Sun or what is more likely, a Sun-like object, giving off heat, appears to be associated with a *falling movement*. Science today tells us the sun obviously does not move in such a fashion so how could so many people mistake the Sun for some other phenomenon? Can Remote Viewing shed some light on what the 50,000 plus witnesses *actually* saw?

The crowd gaze towards the heavens as they observe the promised 'Miracle'

I was first drawn to the idea of using remote viewing to target this strange case after reading Ingo Swann's book *"The Great Apparitions of Mary – An Examination of Twenty-Two Supranormal Appearances"*. There were quite a few remarkable accounts noted in his book, but the Fatima one stood out for me. While Swann was famous as an accomplished pioneer in Remote Viewing, he didn't mention RV in his Marian book. I began to wonder what remote viewing might tell us about the historic events on the 13th October 1917.

The first session presented here was a solo blind Task done by myself in September 2003 early one morning, and pulled from a relatively small target pool of around 250 targets; all placed in brown sealed envelopes, with nothing but reference numbers written on each envelope. I was pretty much fresh out of RV Training so the sessions at the time tended to be very short, with not much detail but they still left a big impression on me. When I eventually opened the feedback envelope, the target description was:

3CA7 – 8410

"Describe The Fatima "event" of October 13th 1917"

"Describe the most important message of the secret of Fatima"

In hindsight this was a poorly written cue, but being new to RV, I was still learning the ropes. Nevertheless, the following sketch, and short summary left me wanting to know more. The Remote Viewing session was a mere 5 pages long, yet each page seemed crammed with relevant data to the tasking. But was it *accurate?*

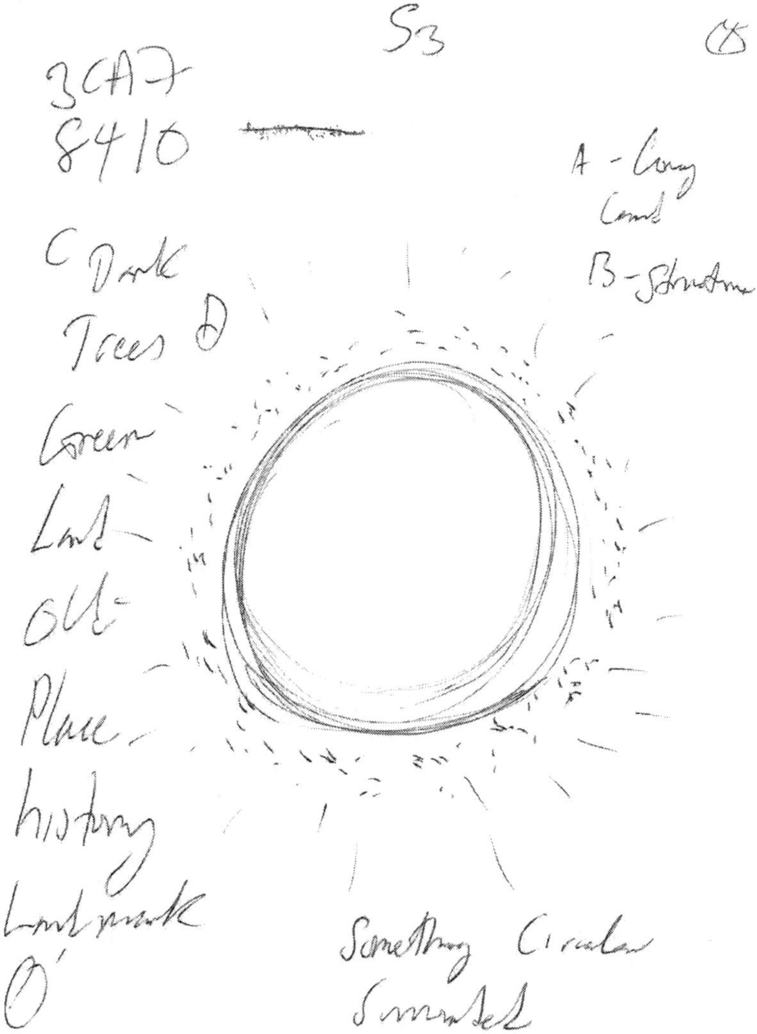

S_3

3CA7
8410

C Dark
Trees D

Green

Land

Old

Place

history

Landmark

O

A - Long
Coast

B - Structure

Something Circular
Surrounded

I had been given a glimpse of *something,* which at least for me, at the time, hinted that maybe there might be something to all this Marian 'stuff'.

It would be over a year before I got another chance to do a blind session on the events at Fatima. This time the target was tasked to me and a few other viewers in my practice group, by an Australian viewer called Elizabeth Ruse. The same data types I had got from my earlier session reappeared once again, but this time with a lot more detail...probably more than I bargained for. There was an overwhelming sensation of a huge light and bright circular object/s in the data, moving and rotating. I also got strange blob like objects, which seemed to be in the air and didn't make any sense at all. The whole session had a very *cosmic* feel to it and I could not shake off the feeling of *"all this weird light "*and where on Earth it came from.

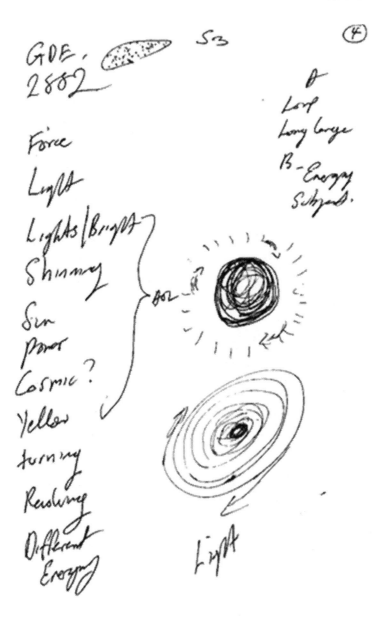

[Transcript] Force, light, Light/Bright, Shinning, Sun, Power, Cosmic?, yellow, Turning, Revolving, Different Energy, Light

O C

S1

Oblong
Emitting
- Dark
Black
Space
Water
Energy
Pulse
Solid
Alive
Hot
Connected
Electric / Blue
Static
Colours / Bright
Red / Brown / Yellow

S2

Specs of light
Dots
Dotty
Spots
high
upward
Swirl
Animal ?
Sign ?
representation
movement

S3

Large
Circle
repeat
revolve
Solid
Subjects
hard to describe
Lots of
Light - blur
main structure /
Person ?
Ball
Round
Oval
Bright

Summary (1)

Hard to identify. Lots of AOL associated with target. Appears to be abstract in some way

Do sense a lot of light at target and a subject is present seems human like, male, very powerful? Long tube like object present giving off light, like a doorway Don't sense anything negative just positive feelings + awareness. Vast space, void and something circular. maybe stars + planets? Also a personal connection to target but who is the male subject at target ??? where is all the light coming from ???

[Open]

Translated text summary format –

"*Hard to identify, Lots of AOL (Analytical Overlay) associated with the target. Appears to be abstract in some way.*

Do sense a lot of light at the target and a subject is present, seems human like, male very powerful? Long tube like object present, giving off light like a doorway. Don't sense anything negative just positive feelings and

awareness. Vast space, void and something circular. Maybe stars &
planets? Also a personal connection to the target but who is the male
subject at target??? **Where is all the light coming from???"**

For the first time, I now *felt* deep down, *something* extraordinary
did indeed occur on that day that totally mesmerized the Cova de
Iria witnesses, based on my two RV sessions and the sessions of
viewers in my group also tasked with the same event by Elizabeth.
As a remote viewer, I had psychically *'felt'* the witnesses utter
bewilderment and awe at this 'light show', whatever it may have
been. I had literally *'felt'* the presence of a bizarre circular or orb-
like object above me, and *'felt'* its movement, and an intense heat
but, I still didn't have a clue as to what it was and crucially from an
RV perspective, I still did not have complete feedback. It was
frustrating to say the least.

I needed more information. My curiosity about the whole thing
had reached fever pitch and I needed a real remote viewing
professional to take a look and see if they could, at the very least,
corroborate what I and many others had been getting over the years
concerning the *Miracle of the Sun* event.

It was suggested I hire the services of **Joseph W. McMoneagle**,
one of the finest remote viewers of our time. I got in contact with
Joe's partner, Nancy 'Scooter' McMoneagle - Chief Operations
Manager for Joe's small company, Intuitive Intelligence
Applications (*IIA*) and I provided the Target ID for Joe to tackle. Joe
as many of you reading this probably already know, works double-
blind (often solo-blind), selecting tasks from a changing collection
prepared for him by someone else. He works alone and he has
absolutely no contact with the target information except via psi. The
target cue was as follows –

"Fatima Apparition, 13 October 1917 in Cova da Iria Fields near Fatima, Portugal."

It took a while to get the results of Joe's viewing due to his existing work commitments, plus there is no way to tell when Joe will happen to pick *my* target from a significant backlog of client targets and from an equally large target pool.

However, on 12th August, 2008 I finally got the results I had been waiting for. It was a surreal moment, as I hurriedly downloaded the file containing the remote viewing data and opened its contents.

The first thing that struck me was the level of detail presented in Joe's report. It was packed full of relevant information about the target and the summary report was concise and to the point. It even included a map and a coloured sketch as well. Here, presented for the first time, is the full report.

[Note: Again please bear in mind what you are about to read was done with the viewer having no idea what even the nature of the target was, under fully double-blind science-derived controlled conditions. All Joe had to work with was the task reference number.]*

TARGET: T72108

Please describe the target.

The target is described as follows:

"My sense is that I'm standing on a hill side which is not quite as large as a mountain, but significantly larger than the surrounding hills. This particular hill is in the center of a lot of hills. It has a ridgeline which runs approximately from the north-northwest down toward the south-southeast. My sense is there is a village located near this ridgeline toward the north and west of hill peak. The location of the event is just below this ridgeline at the edge of the village location. Today there is a larger, more modern city that has been built along the main highway at the foot of this hill and village.

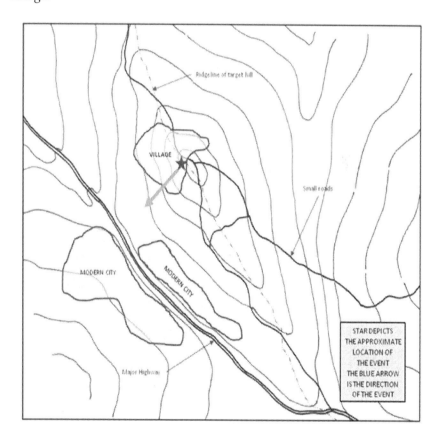

The approximate location of the event appears to have occurred facing what looks like a rocky ledge or series of ledges rising to the ridgeline. The actual event occurred in the direction of the blue arrow or to the southwest of where it was observed from.

My sense is that there were a lot of people present at this event location, specifically when the event occurred. I get a sense that these people gathered because of previous occurrences and were now gathered because of the possibility of another.

The visibility was very poor. I am getting an impression that it is raining, heavily overcast with dark and ominous clouds, with lots of fog or low hanging clouds obscuring the area. The air is cold, but not freezing. This apparently has little effect on the crowd gathered to see what might happen.

The event takes place in the very early afternoon [2-4 PM]. I get an impression that hundreds [if not thousands] of people are gathered here to watch some kind of an event. They all seem to be peering upward and toward the southwest.

There are breaks in the heavy cloud cover which everyone seems to be peering directly at and some are even pointing with their hands raised in the air. Apparently there is something within the cloud cover that everyone is staring at and watching.

It almost appears to be some kind of an almost silent explosion or event of some kind that is triggering a large expanse of light which is filling the sky. Very bright light is expanding downward through the breaks in the heavy and dark cloud cover.

*Apparently this is some sort of high altitude cosmic event, probably not unlike the high altitude meteor explosion at **Tunguska**, Russia; or the one that occurred October 4th, 2002 over Siberia[17].*

*It looks like a **medium sized meteor** of approximately 120,000 tons entering the upper atmosphere at an approximate angle of 33+ degrees, and moving at an astounding speed – I would estimate at approximately 20-25 miles per second [or about, 72,000-90,000 mph. Heat build-up within the object was instantaneous, causing it to vaporize at approximately 80,000 feet or 15+ miles above the surface, creating an **intense and explosive release of light,** essentially becoming a **miniature Sun** for approximately 20-30 seconds. Changes in the Earth's atmosphere [normal upper atmospheric air condensed into vapour] created a huge shift in polarization, creating a massive circular rainbow for approximately 30 seconds following the release of light. The light show in this event must have been incredible. The shockwave from this event was probably mediated to some extent by the altitude and lack of atmospheric density."*

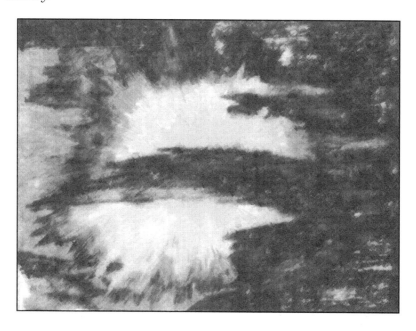

Above – As seen through the heavy cloud cover
The original Joe McMoneagle sketch of the 'event'

The entire event probably took about one minute or less. The rainbow effect probably stayed visible for at least ten minutes after the burst of light. Anyone looking directly at the event at the time would have been temporarily blinded by the light even though it was partially hidden.

JWM\RV 1.5 hrs. August 12, 2008

We now have remote viewing data from at least one RV professional which seems to suggest the events of that day, did indeed take place, but I suspect many framed the meteorological spectacle in a religious and mystical context, and reasonably mistook the bright orb in the sky for the Sun itself. The matter would have had a much richer context for evaluation if given the benefit of analysis on the many viewing sessions I have seen on this target to date, including Joe's contributions. However, the story does not end there.

There is still the baffling and bizarre reason why so many people ended up at the one single location where a rare event such as was witnessed at Fatima.

Fatima – The Forgotten ESP Connection

Many may not be aware that the events of that miraculous day appear to have been *predicted* several months before Lúcia Santos and her cousins Jacinta and Francisco Marto had their first encounters with the mysterious Lady of Light on the 13th May 1917. The day that would change the lives of these young seers, and indeed Catholics around the globe for generations to come. As you will see, it would appear others were looking forward to this special day, a day that would go down in history.

Carlos Calderon was a member of a group of mediums and spiritualists who met regularly to engage in the art of *'Automatic Writing'* a common practice amongst popular occultist of that era especially throughout Europe and South America. Various mystical 'orders' flourished and actively tried to engage in direct communication with the astral plane and non-human entities.

On February 7th according to Carlos, that evening during a normal meeting, one of the members of the group received a *'message'* via automatic writing. The message was written by an assistant from 'right to left' so the only way you could decipher its content, was to hold it in front of a mirror, or through a bright light so one could read its contents *through* the page.

The message gave advanced notice that something of a transcendental nature would occur 3 months later, on the 13th day of May, that year.

Here is an excerpt of the message:

"It is not our custom to predict the future. The mystery of the future is impenetrable, though at times God permits a corner of the veil to be lifted over that which it covers. Have confidence in our prophecy.

The day of May 13th *will be one of great happiness for the good Souls of the world. Have faith and be good. Ego Sum Charitas ["I am love"]*

Always at your side, we are here as your friends to help guide your steps and assist in your work. The brilliant light of the morning star will illuminate the path.

- Stella Matutina"[18]

Transcript taken from *A Ray of Light on Fatima* published in 1974 by Filipe Furtado de Mendonca

By the end of the meeting the group decided to document the event and also place an advert in a popular Portuguese Lisbon newspaper, *Diara de Noticias*. The subsequent prediction was successfully published on **10th March 1917** in the paper under a small column simply titled '**135917**' (cipher for 13th May, 1917)

Another 'psychic' group also published yet another prediction in not just one but several newspapers in Porto and the whole of Portugal with the following announcement released on 11th May:

Mr. Editor:

13TH May 1917

On this day as predicted by several members of a spiritualist group, a revelation about the war will occur, which will strongly impress the world.

I am a Spiritualist and dedicated propagandist of Truth.

ANTONIO.

A guerra e o espiritismo

Revelação sensacional

Recebemos hontem um postal.

cujo texto passamos a reprodu-
zir:
Porto, 11 de Maio de 1917.
Srs. Redactores:
Foi participado pelos Espiritos,
a diversos grupos espiritas, que
no dia treze do corrente, hade
dar-se um facto, a respeito da
guerra, que impressionará forte-
mente toda a gente.
Tenho a honra de me subscre-
ver, Espirita e dedicado propa-
gandista da verdade.—Antonio.»

According to Fatima researchers, Dr Joaquim Fernandez and Fina D' Armada they had this to say about the strange press releases from the psychics:

"Someone or something identifying itself as 'Stella Matutina' announced to the Portuguese people that something important would happen on May 13, 1917. The information coming from somewhere, expressed in the form of a cipher, was picked up by a group of psychics in Lisbon, during one of their regular meetings. This group deemed it important enough to pay for the cost of publicizing it in a local newspaper paper"[19]

I did some research on the name or term *Stella Matutina* and it appears to an initiatory magical order. Whether this group or splinter lodge had anything to do with the Portuguese psychics has not been verified but still the reference to the **Morning Star** (Venus) in the original automatic writing message is intriguing to say the least given its links to orders and lodges such as Freemasonry and the Hermetic Order of the Golden Dawn - both quite active at the time.

Dr Joaquim Fernandez and Fina D' Armada further add:

*"In the wake of the historic events in Fatima, it would appear that the group of psychics in Lisbon, which had received precognitive information that something **important**, would happen on that fateful day, lost a "war" of its own, one waged upon it by the dominant culture. With no benefit to be derived from a "psychic" interpretation of the phenomenon, at least not in the short term, they retreated into the woodwork and the day of great happiness" turned out not to be so – at least not for them [psychics]"*[20]

Few would disagree with their conclusions. The situation has not improved 97 years later for Remote Viewers and decent Psychics today with psychic research and acceptance at an all-time low. Although there are signs things may be about to change.

It appears to me someone somewhere clearly had *'advanced'* notice of what would occur on the fields of Cova de Iria on 13th October 1917. I can see no other explanation that would explain why 60,000 plus people would find themselves directly above such a light display at the *right time* and the *right place.*

As a side note, and long after Joe had finally been given feedback for his target, I asked Joe via email, how in the world did the children know about the impending 'light show'? His answer was they could have come about the same information as any good intuitive or psychic would have. That sounds like a reasonable explanation but I suspect we may never know for sure.

It would also appear the Catholic Church at the time had no interest whatsoever in these numerous psychic press releases of something important going down, until this day, and yet, on **May**

119

13th **1917** as predicted by the psychics, an apparition of a small "lady", a being of light would *initiate* what many would undoubtedly declare to be the most significant Marian Apparition of the 20th century which continues to *greatly impress the entire world.*

In closing, here are some questions serious researchers into The Fatima apparition may want to consider pursuing further:

- How did the children *know* about the impending cosmic/meteorological events that would occur that day?

- Who was the mysterious Lady of light (who by the way, *never* introduced herself as 'Mary' or was identified as such by any of the seers)

- Why were adverts placed in several prominent Portuguese newspapers of the time by 'psychics' predicting an event that would *"Greatly impress the entire world"* commence on the day the children began contact with the *'Lady of Light'*?

- Who or *what* was in contact with these psychics?

- Who exactly were these psychics?

- Why is the Vatican heavily involved in tracking *NEO's (Near Earth Objects)* and funding state-of the-art Observatories around the globe?

- Was the alleged Third Secret and indeed the entire 'Miracle' no more than a dire warning of how vulnerable our planet is to sudden and unannounced global catastrophe from a rogue meteorite?

As always, it's extremely important to bear in mind with cases such as these, regardless of the thousands of witnesses to the 'miracle' and sworn testimony, we do not have *full* feedback for all the events and remote viewing data submitted in this report. However I would like to think we may have at last shed some light on what really happened in the skies above Cova de Iria 97 years ago as we approach the 100th anniversary of *The Miracle of The Sun.*

CHAPTER 8
The Carlos Diaz Photos - UFO Case #2

"Lie to a liar, for lies are his coin; Steal from a thief, for that is easy; lay a trap for a trickster and catch him at first attempt, but beware of an honest man"

- ***An old Arab quote***

C arlos Diaz Martinez, a photographer and film maker by profession, who made wedding videos for locals in his community, made a presentation in 1997 at the 2nd UFO Congress which took place in Acapulco, Mexico. He shared with the audience tales of his experience and encounters with Plasma-like space craft, shaped like a typical flying saucer in Tepoztlan, Mexico from 1981 to 1993.

The astonishing photographs of bright glowing orange/golden saucer -like objects, stunned the UFO community at the time and was subsequently featured in numerous documentaries, including the now famous *"Ships of Light"* produced by German researcher, Michael Hesemann.

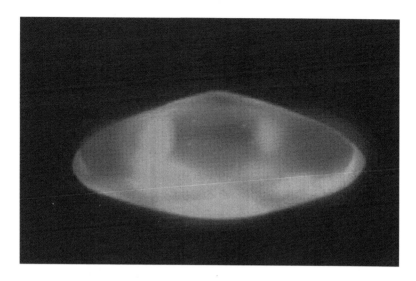

So what was this strange object filmed and photographed by Carlos Diaz? Where did it come from? How was it made? This was one of those photographs which looked just too good to be true and I really wanted to know whether this was a real extraterrestrial event or something else entirely.

It was time to find out once and for all.

I gave the target to two sets of viewers. One was the Aurora Group as a routine practice target which none of them were aware of and was done under double blind conditions by several team viewers.

The other viewer was Joe McMoneagle.

The Tasking:

I contacted IIA *(Intuitive Intelligence Applications)*, Joe's remote viewing company, and gave the Project Manager, Nancy McMoneagle, the details of the project.

From the start, I was impressed with the friendly service and high level of professionalism and was assured the target would be completed under *double blind* conditions which means nobody with any information about the task would be around Joe at the time of the viewing.

Nancy placed the photograph of the UFO Carlos Diaz allegedly took, into an envelope, sealed it and gave it the target reference number **5908**. She then wrote on the outside of the envelope the following tasking:

TARGET 5908

1) Please define the target

2) Give the purpose of the target and

3) Origins of the target.

As ever, Joe would be kept blind to the target and will know nothing about it until he receives his feedback (after all questions have been asked about it based on Joe's original data) ONLY THEN WILL THE ENVELOPE BE OPENED AND THE TARGET REVEALED.

[This will be the standard procedure for all subsequent projects.]

124

The envelope is then placed in a pile of existing sealed envelopes full of targets; all left for Joe to eventually remote view them. As a result, there would often be weeks, or even months, before I would get a response as Joe works a hectic schedule and was also semi-retired from doing operational RV work for clients, so I was always grateful he had found enough time to work my projects.

I didn't have long to wait as it turned out, and several weeks later, I got an email in my inbox. It was from Nancy; she had good news!

The information I was looking for had finally arrived. I opened the file containing the data, and read the contents slowly.

Here is the actual remote viewing data produced by Joe in full and in its original format.

TARGET: 5908

1. Please define the Target.

2. What is the purpose of the Target?

3. Describe the Origins of the Target.

The Target is defined as follows:

An inverted and colorful, slightly warped or melted cone of hardened plastic or fiberglass, suspended from a cord of connective white light fiber, possibly hung from a suspension cable or horizontal feature of some kind. Cone is oval in shape around its lower edges and approximately two feet wide at its narrowest point and approximately three feet wide at its widest point. It appears to be bright red along its lowest edge fading into yellows, reds, browns, and blacks, all interweaving as it rises through the cone shape eventually fading into a brown to dusky black then totally black at its upper folds.

Lighting is dramatic and artful, vis' a vis white light fiber cord which extends downward to the top of the art form, connecting there. It causes light to stream both through and onto the inner segments of the cone shape. There does not appear to be any light on the exterior of the form at all.

I get the impression that this is some kind of an Art Form. It is very delicate in nature and easily broken. It is or has been created by someone to impress those who look upon it both for its intrinsic beauty as well as its representation of color and light. It is mesmerizing in how it is being displayed. It is being displayed in such a way as to capture the imagination of those who see it. It has been hung in such a way to completely capture the audience who might see it in its full display.

It is very beautiful. It is a very wonderful demonstration and eye catching.

[See drawing attached]

The purpose of the target is:

Its purpose is to sell an idea or a concept. It was made to demonstrate a concept or an idea which is important to someone. It demonstrates something that is possible in a larger concept, something that this person wants to sell. I have a sense that the customer wants to know if the object is genuine.

*This art object is **not** genuine; it is a copy of the original.*

<u>*The origins of the target are:*</u>

Glass artist's shop somewhere south of the border, probably somewhere in an area south-southeast of Mexico City; approximately 20-26 kilometers from the borders of Mexico City proper.

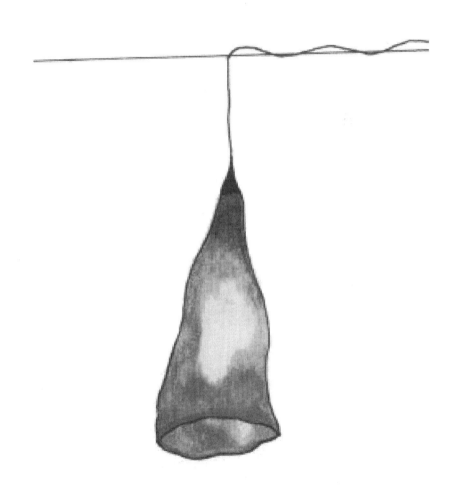

Fig 1. Counterfeit Art Object

JWM\ RV 1.5 Hrs.\ May 27, 2008

I was disappointed to say the least, but at the same time, we had a new source of information regarding the Diaz case, which corroborates counter claims made about the authenticity of the footage. Also, the Aurora Group data supported the idea the photo was probably a fake or at the very least, man-made.

Here are extracts from Bill Hamilton, a researcher who investigated the case in response to growing claims of a possible hoax;

"Carlos Diaz is a pleasant fellow and friendly enough, however to support the message posted by Scott Corrales I would like to say that I had the opportunity to examine the footage he brought to Village Labs when he was in the company of Michael Hesseman.

When Jim Diletosso loaded the footage into the computer and we started stepping through the frames as well as playing it at various speeds, I noticed that the so-called plasma craft, looking like a **Japanese hanging lamp**, *descended in a jerky motion as if it were being lowered by rope or cable. The interior illumination of this object is static (unlike other UFO illumination) and doesn't change in position or intensity. When the wind blows nearby branches, the plasma ship also shakes in the wind as if it were a light object. The so-called firing of a laser beam from near the bottom side of the object appears like a small focused flashlight beam.*

Our conclusion, also based on the fact that Carlos does video work and films weddings and celebrations, is that his video of the plasma ship is most likely a hoax using a small model.

Sincerely,

Bill Hamilton"[21]

Further damning critics of the Carlos Diaz case came from two other researchers, Scott Corrales and Pascal Lopresti:

"Carlos Diaz has always refused to allow the video to be analyzed by any of Mexico's researchers or from anywhere else in the world, arguing that he doesn't trust any researcher... My opinion in this regard is that I definitely doubt that there is any truth to the video.

First: Because he has not allowed it to be subjected to laboratory analysis.

Second: He leaves his house to film the UFO and doesn't have a tripod. He then states that the tripod was lent to him by the aliens ("his friends").

Third: No human being from this planet can board a plasma ship with his/her physical body and a camcorder."

"As a researcher, I feel obligated to make this event known to the public, and to let the public draw its own conclusions. My own conclusions as a researcher of this type of event are that it is not only false, but also utterly ridiculous.

I truly regret that persons like Carlos Diaz should go around telling tales of this nature, since in my opinion, they are solely interested in attracting fame and money by calling themselves "contactees" and it troubles me, more than anything, because these attitudes promote skepticism among those who seek clear and truthful answers."

Pascal Lopresti UFO Researcher[22]

[Translation (c) 2000. Scott Corrales/Institute of Hispanic Ufology Special Thanks to Dr Virgilio Sánchez Ocejo]

This demonstrates why Remote Viewing of UFOs can be a very tricky business indeed and I would advocate only advanced remote viewers attempt doing such targets because a less experienced viewer could easily pick up the *'idea'* behind the trickery and allow their imagination to run wild with the data, seeing extraterrestrial flying 'ships of light' where there are none. At the same time, as comprehensive as Joe's data may be, there is still no real feedback since Diaz has yet to denounce his photo as a fraud. The primary purpose of including this data is to demonstrate how easy it may be for even so called experts to be fooled by a determined hoaxer and to not rush into believing something just because it looks impressive or be swayed by glossy presentations masked in potential trickery and deception.

This unfortunately would be the first of many false starts in the hunt for real genuine extraterrestrial space craft and a valuable lesson learned in knowing what type of UFO targets to pick in order to sort out the wheat from the chaff.

CHAPTER 9

The Lincolnshire Wind Turbine Mystery
UFO Case #3

T his next case would simply have been a routine target without any UFO associations, but I have decided to include this to demonstrate yet again, how difficult it can be for remote viewers to distinguish between *real events* at a target that may not seem so clear cut and the potential to reach the wrong conclusions without full feedback. For now, I hope someday we will be proven right, but as always in cases such as the one you are about to read, no firm conclusions should be reached without the availability of full and accurate feedback.

I received an email from one of my fellow Aurora Group remote viewers Marv Darley, about a project he was about to start and how he needed some remote viewing volunteers to help him out. I was not really in the mood to do any viewing, but decided to participate all the same. Marv is also the moderator of remote viewing's largest online database of sessions and forums on the internet called TKR Ten Thousand Roads and one of *the best* viewers I have had the pleasure to work with over the years. (I have hidden Marv's true name to protect him as he wishes to keep his professional life separate from the world of Remote Viewing.)

As usual, all the viewers who responded to Marv's plea for help, including myself, were given absolutely no information whatsoever regarding the target. All we had to work on was the following random target reference numbers:

8719 - 1771

I remember doing an initial ERV session (Extended Remote Viewing), which, when done properly, can give the viewer a more detailed or *deeper* contact with the target. I was still experimenting with the method and thought it would be a good time to do an operational target which could be corroborated and independently analysed by someone other than myself.

It was during the ERV session I noticed *something* very peculiar about the target, which made no sense to me whatsoever at the time, but kept repeating itself over and over again.

The following day I sat down in front of my desk and proceeded with the tasking to see if I could make sense of my impressions of the previous night using the TDS Method.

Here is the complete session data in its entirety.

PIR xx-x   ES OK   Tumor
DB   PS OK   19-01-08
NM   (Pm)

8719   T
1771

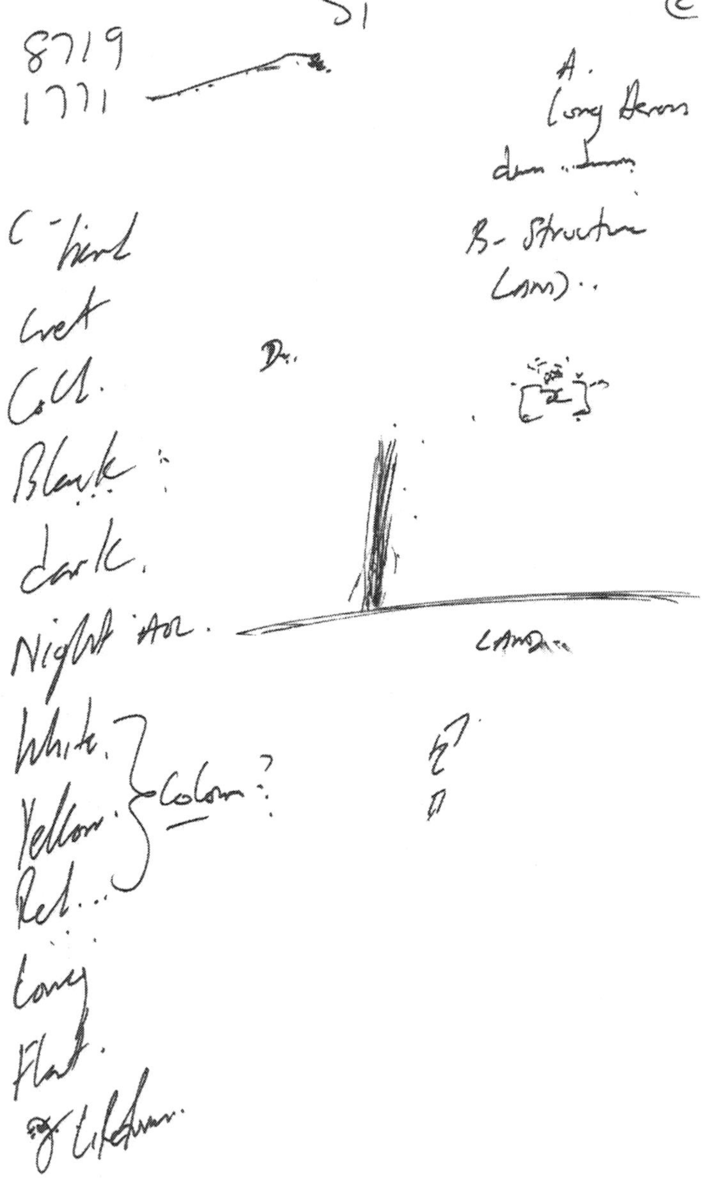
S1
8719
1771
A.
B- Structure
Cold.
Black
dark.
Night Air.
LAND...
White.
Yellow.
Red...
Colour?
Long
Flat.

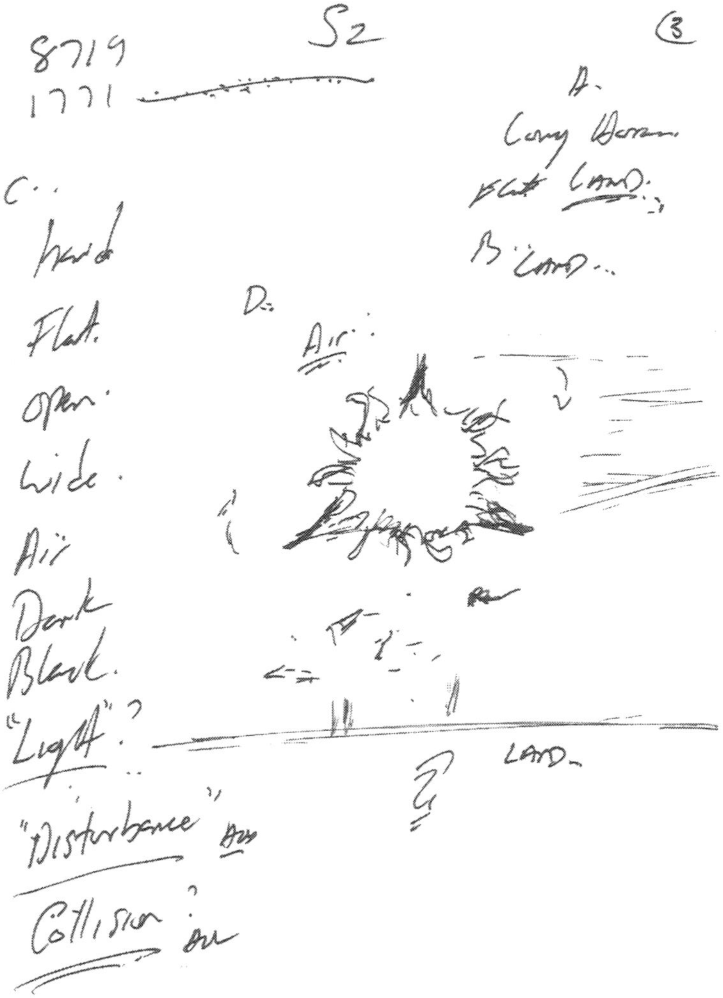

8719
1771

S2

③

A.
Long Horizon
Flat Land.

B. Land...

C..
hard

Flat.

open.

Wide.

Air

Dark

Black.

"Light"?

"Disturbance" Aw

Collision? Aw

D.:
Air:

LAND.

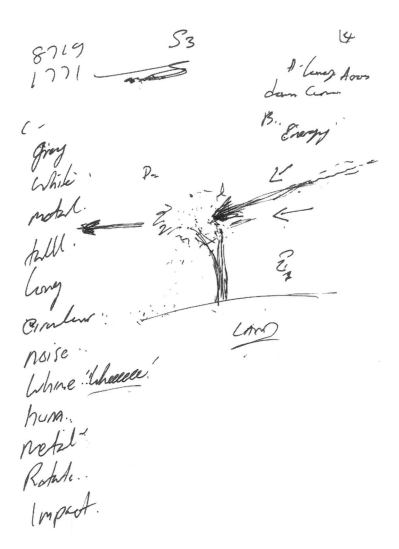

Transcript – Grey, White, Metal, Tall, Long, Circular, Noise, Whine 'Wheeee', hum, metal, Rotate, Impact.

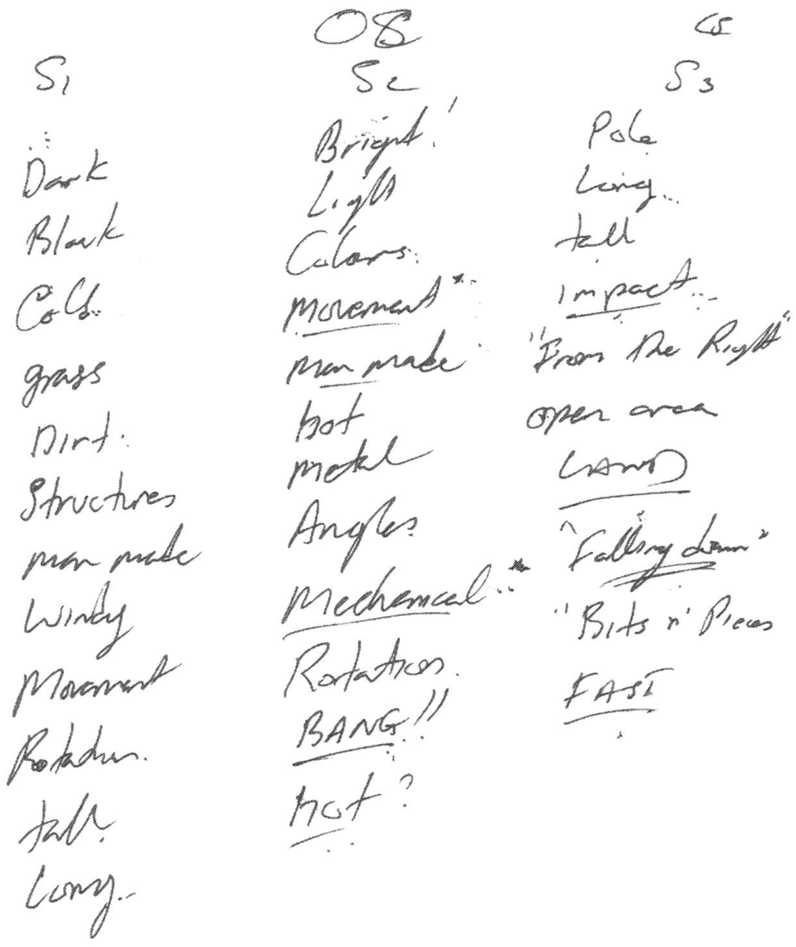

[Handwritten notes across three columns]

S1
Dark
Black
Cold
grass
Dirt
Structures
man made
Windy
Movement
Rotation
tall
long

OS
S2
Bright
Light
Colors:
Movement
man made
hot
metal
Angles
Mechanical
Rotation
BANG!!
hot?

S3
Pole
long
tall
impact
"From the Right"
open area
LAND
"Falling down"
"Bits n' Pieces
FAST

S1- Dark, Black, Cold, Grass, Dirt, Structures, man-made, windy, Movement, Rotation, Tall, Long. **S2 -** Bright, light, Colours, Movement, Man-made, hot metals, angles, mechanical, Rotation, **BANG!!,** hot? **S3 –** Pole, long, tall, impact, "from the right", open area, LAND, falling down, "Bits and pieces", **FAST**

MATRIX

S	D	E	A₁	E₁	P	A₂
			odd.	Lights		helicopter
Structure:			noise.	Movement.		Plane,
Dark.		Rotation	Crash,	Airbourne		windmill
Black.			Bang.		Metal.	
			"Accident"		Rockets	
	Sparks.		"Crashing".		Wings.	
	Crash?		Debris		Man made.	
	Impact.		Twisted.			
	Star like Shape.		wreckage.			
			Sparks			

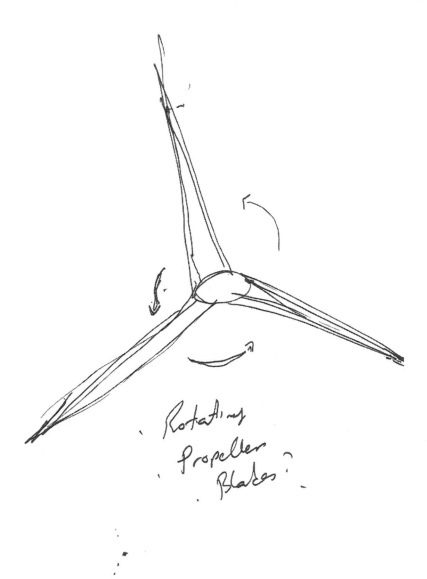

Rotating
Propeller
Blades?

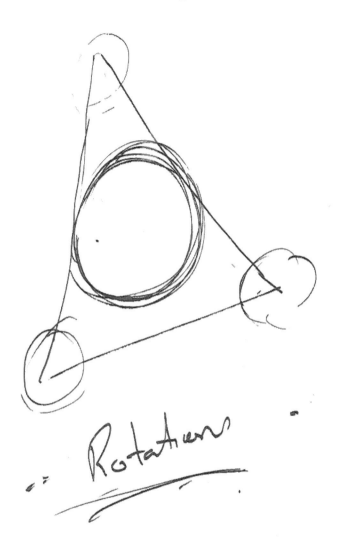

Rotations

Sr

STRUCTURE .

— movement
— rotates.
— Propeller.
— Judder :.
— Break.
— LARGE
— WHITE
— Metal.
— man made.
— mechanical

S5

LIGHTS/HEAS

: Object.

- metal.

- Airborne.

- Plane/Helicopter?

- Collision.

- Accident:

- DARK / NIGHT.

- Cold.

Summary.

TARGET FEELS LIKE ITS IN AN OPEN SPACE AREA. LOTS OF LAND AND SURROUNDED BY TALL POLE-LIKE OBJECTS.

THERE IS "ROTATION" ASSOCIATED WITH THIS OBJECT SLOW MOVING NOT SURE WHAT THE POLE IS FOR BUT ALSO THERE IS SOMETHING ELSE PRESENT AT THE TARGET. A "COLLUSION" OR IMPACT OF SOME KIND WHICH LEAVES BITS OF WRECKAGE ALL OVER THE PLACE.

As you can see, it was all very bizarre and as always with data like this, it's impossible to know what you have produced until you are shown some feedback. As a general rule, Aurora targets were supposed to feature only targets with absolute feedback, so I was confident it was not ET related, as we wanted to do things the right way and in protocol, so we can measure accuracy against known targets which would have come in handy once we began working targets for clients.

Nevertheless, I scanned the data into a PDF file format and emailed it off to Marv for analysis. I was convinced the session would be a complete miss yet at the same time, still intrigued about the repeated rotations and strange triangle pattern that kept popping up during the session.

We didn't have to wait too long as it turned out and on the 21st of January, we received our feedback.

To say I was surprised would be an understatement:

8719-1771

"DAMAGED WIND TURBINE – LINCOLNSHIRE

CORNISHOLME FEN - LOUTH"

4th January 2009

The **BBC** released the news of the damage the following day:

"Blade falls off wind farm turbine"

Engineers are investigating why a blade more than 20 metres (66ft) long fell off a wind turbine in Lincolnshire.

It is believed the blade came away from one of the 20 turbines at Conisholme Fen near Louth early on Sunday.

Ecotricity, *which operates the site, said the turbines manufacturers were on site and assessing the damage.*

A spokesman said the turbines were in a very isolated location and there was no danger to property or the public. An inspection is due to be carried out.

The spokesperson added: **"This has never happened before so we really have no idea what might have gone wrong."**

"We will conduct a thorough inspection of the turbines to see if there is a problem and put it right."

Well that answered a few questions as to why I kept getting windmill-like propellers going round and round in circles.

However, the story gets even weirder at this point. It turns out the other viewers also got very strange data including, but not limited to; a collision, airborne devices, military or secret cover ups and monitoring over the target area. They also picked up a strange odd looking triangular craft or object which seemed to have collided with the wind turbine. Were we *all* mistaken? Where did the strange craft come from? Had the remote viewers simply mistaken the turbines three propeller's as a separate triangular object?

It turns out there was more to the story than was first reported in the media.

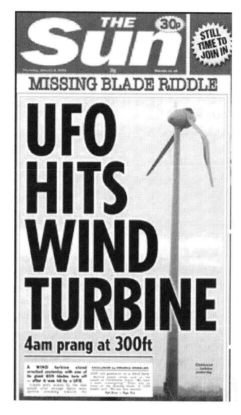

"UFO Hits Wind Turbine – The Sun"

The UK press went crazy with the initial story of a UFO damaging the wind turbine and it even made front page news on some of the biggest newspapers in the land, with reports of flying lights in the sky in the vicinity of the Wind farm, which were later dismissed as a local firework display which occurred earlier that same night.

A month later, Ecotricity, the firm responsible for the wind farms, put out a report saying they had finally figured out what caused one of the blades to fall off and another blade looking completely mangled - Their answer? *"Loose bolts"* and *"mechanical fatigue"* of the blades were to blame. There had been no collision according to their detailed analysis of what went wrong.

147

There the story would have died except for the inexplicable and quite often shocking UFO sightings and reports by the residents living around the Louth region and all over the county of Lincolnshire that continues to this day.

What was *not* reported in the media when the story first broke out, was the very specific sightings of strange UFOS with tentacle-like lights, hovering over the wind farm, seen by several eye witnesses as well as *flying Triangles* (looking **EXACTLY** like the one I clearly described in my session).

Richard D Hall, a well-known UK based UFO researcher and TV presenter, has done a huge amount of research on the subject, and located many of these witnesses who over the years, have seen hundreds of sightings of Black, 40 foot *Triangles* making impossible manoeuvres over the same area as the wind farm and within other areas of Lincolnshire. Indeed the area has now been dubbed *The Lincolnshire Triangle* due to the abundance of mysterious activity including, but not limited to; animal mutilations, unexplained aerial phenomenon and animal abductions.

UFO Witness, Morag Taylor from Alford

Morag Taylor claimed she saw a **Black Triangle** and gave specific descriptions of the object the night she witnessed it[23].

One witness, Morag Taylor, described seeing black triangles within the area. Her descriptions match those of **Eric Goring,** who has also witnessed strange looking black triangles flying over Brinkhill, near Louth, as far back as 2008; just a few months before the damaged Wind Turbine incident and again, within the Lincolnshire Triangle zone.[24]

Goring claims he has seen *hundreds* of these craft making incredible manoeuvres at night, and on one particular night, he claimed to have seen over **40** such craft over Brinkhill!

In a 2008 interview with the Louth Leader Newspaper Goring had this to say –

"I have been watching these space ships for six weeks now, and saw eight together on September 25th and more again last night. It was really spooky and I can say for sure that any explanation these are just Chinese lanterns is ridiculous."

Recounting his latest sighting, he said: *"I was outside on my scooter at around 5am and watched them until about 6am. One came from the front and then others came in from different directions.*

"They seemed to be lighting the clouds up as they went along and their lights were bright white. There was no noise and they moved slowly, hovering and then shooting off at speed."

Mr Goring described the objects as ***triangular in shape*** and lined with lights. He drew these diagrams to illustrate what he saw, explaining: *"I estimate they were around 50 feet across in size and sometimes they shone a large searchlight from the bottom."*

Eric revealed he had a close encounter with one of the objects last month [2008]: *"I saw one come from the direction of the fields and over a tree. I almost walked right under it as it was just hovering in the air about 200 feet above me.*

"It wasn't shining its search line down but I didn't want to go too near it as I was worried about radiation."

Notice the uncanny similarity between the description below of what Goring saw and the remote viewing sketch.

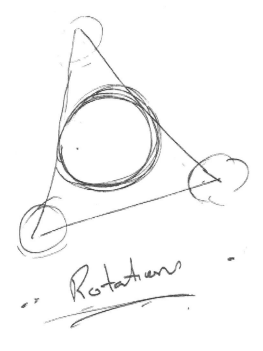

RV Data of a flying triangle very similar to those witnessed all over Lincolnshire or Properller blades of the wind turbine ?

Goring, in an interview with Richard D Hall, describes *the triangle* as often appearing as a round glowing yellow light with the 3

pointed corners showing around the edges which is exactly what I drew in my session.

Below is a report from the Louth Local Newspaper back in 2008 (again it's important to emphasize this was published *before* the wind turbine incident which occurred in January 2009)

UFO investigator backs triangle 'spacecraft' claims

Wednesday 11.30am - BRINKHILL'S 'alien spacecraft' enthusiast Eric Goring, may be on to something, according to an independent UFO investigator.

After reading the Leader's story on Mr Goring's extraordinary claims last week, a local UFO investigator has been to the village to scan the skies himself.

The man, who asked not to be named, said: "I can now report I have been to Brinkhill twice and on both occasions myself, and a friend have seen the objects. I must say they are as Mr Goring described.

"I saw three objects with lights on each point of the triangle with a very large central light. The larger object flew within a hundred feet of my car and we experienced total electrical mayhem and I felt charged with static.

The objects are definitely not the Aurora Black project plane because it uses pulse-scram jet engines and these were silent and we estimated they covered the distance from the coast to the Wolds in around a second - and that is not possible even for Aurora.

"The objects are able to disguise themselves when needed because the large one made its black fuselage vanish on more than one occasion. It did not turn out its lights so we could clearly see it. When it appeared as an object, not just lights, it astonished me!"

The man described how, on a following night, he witnessed several fighter planes flying on afterburner "with no navigation lights on." He said: "In my opinion, this was to debunk the reports and to provide an explanation for the orange glowing spheres also sighted recently. What we saw was not the orange objects.

"I have contacted BUFORA (British UFO Research Association] and MUFON (Mutual UFO Network] with the information and I am trying

154

to get hold of some decent cameras to document it as we are setting up an overnight watch on the weekend."

He added: "This is a unique opportunity to capture something extraordinary on film that may help with the disclosure project."[25]

It remains to be seen whether one of these *Flying Triangles* was responsible for the damaged wind turbine and we have to conclude there is no evidence to suggest this is indeed the case given Ecotriciti's excuses for the rare '*It's-never-happened before*' turbine damage, but on the other hand, when one considers the odd night time Air Force surveillance overlooking the entire Lincolnshire Triangle region, noticeably over RAF Digby and its equally weird observation tower locals claim the Air Force use purely for climbing up and sleeping inside the platforms 'overnight' – You do begin to wonder what it is exactly they are *observing* over this well-known notorious UFO hotspot? See photo of the Tower and its platforms. Note this is not a radio tower. There may be a more plausible explanation for the platforms as the Aerial Erector School AES is also based at nearby RAF Digby, so the platforms could simply be training rigs for students.

I should also mention that other different types of craft have been spotted in recent years in the surrounding area, including a terrifying case where a father and his two children, witnessed a huge gigantic metallic egg shaped ufo while travelling in their car from Althorpe towards Mablethorpe in Lincolnshire. *(Within the Lincolnshire Triangle)* The car in front of them also stopped, as the object silently came to a halt in the middle of the road, right in front of them, literally blocking out the sky line due to its enormous size. It came from the east (coast line) and then just shot off at an impossible speed leaving the witnesses daughter screaming and his son shocked at what they had just seen. See recreated image courtesy of Richard D Hall.

Photo curtesy of Richard D Hall ©copyright

In that same month of September 2011, one of the biggest mysteries yet to hit Lincolnshire would occur with the unexplained overnight abduction of over 1500 sheep from a locked and secure farm without a trace. A mystery that remains unsolved to this day.

News   Sport   Lifestyle   Community

Published on **Wednesday 14 December 2011 15:11**

Latest UFO sighting off Mablethorpe coast fuels talk of extra-terrestrial life

So what do we make of these reports of flying triangles presumably invading the skies over Lincolnshire at will. I do not believe these are extraterrestrial in origin, at least not the Flying Triangle. I suspect they may be man-made. According to one expert on the subject, Julian Schmidt, who made the following comments in the Louth Leader:

"I have been studying these Black Triangle phenomena since 1987, when my three sons and I witnessed one flying low and slow across our house one night. I distinctly heard a low pitched humming sound being made by the craft.

The sound reminded me of a 600 amp 60 hertz transformer under maximum load. I am an Electronic Technician and have experience with state of the art technology.

It is my belief that these craft use some sort of fusion reactor that must be shielded with a very powerful electromagnetic field. Similar to the Tokamak Fusion [26]technology.

I do not believe that these craft are piloted by alien beings. This technology may also be able to cancel the effects of gravity and drag. Hence the incredible rates of acceleration.

A friend of mine has a brother working for the NSA. All he will tell me is that they have technology 20 years in advance of what we civilians have access to.

I believe the United States operates these Black Triangles. It is not so hard to imagine when you consider their annual military budget is nearly 600 billion dollars!"

What this particular project highlighted was the difficulty an analyst or viewer faces when there is little or no feedback. I am not 100% certain my rotating triangle was not mistaken for the windmill's turbine propellers, even if flying triangles were spotted in the vicinity. For now, this case remains inconclusive and needs much more feedback before any real remote viewing conclusions can be made regarding the cause of the extensive damage to the turbine.

Our hunt for the elusive *extraterrestrial* continues as we explore deeper the symbiotic connection between UFO'S and classified Black Budget technologies which *appear* to be out of this world.

AURORA GROUP ANALYSIS REPORT
FOR RV PROJECT 8719 – 1771

METHOD OF ANALYSIS
By Marv Darley

Sessions were collated and solid data assimilated into tabular form (see next page).Recurrent data is highlighted by an increase in font size and thickness. Whilst this by no means presents a 100% summation of the groups' data it nevertheless pulls together all the key themes and concepts into one readily digestible format.

Readers are advised to study individual sessions and in particular sketches, which are not included here.

ANALYST'S SUMMARY O F EVENT for 8719/1771

On 4TH *January 2009 in Conisholme, Lincolnshire (UK) a wind turbine was struck and damaged by a low flying object. The object was manmade, terrestrial in origin, and linked through design and intention to a secretive group of people, most probably belonging to or with strong ties to the military.*

The object appears to have been manned and the cause of the collision human error (due to fatigue). The collision triggered a panic and a need to calm the situation; time was of the essence.

The collision was witnessed by a group of people present, and watching at the time, in a nearby van.

The flying object (and cause of the crash) itself was designed for surveillance purposes and is cutting edge technology. It was most probably triangular in shape. On the night of the collision it was engaged in a test exercise.

Marv Darley 21/1/09

LIFEFORMS	EMOTION	ENERGY
Successful GROUP	Calm a situation	Swooping
tired	Time of essence	Disturbance
sporty		Collision
one representing many		Impact
good intentions		
Macro view		
Highly educated		
Powerful Secretive		
Official base		

OBJECTS	CONCEPTS	STRUCTURES
Appropriate gear Kidney shaped object **van** communication device **machine** bank of controls being inside **triangular object** Flying vehicle	Synchronise Magnify Doped Competitive field **Surveillance** Stealth Space between bodies Earth rise Accident Cutting edge	**Tall thin structures** outside road windmills military installation

SENSORIES	INTENT	ONE LIFEFORM
	How far will it go?	Inner push
Cold	Mutual benefit of	**Tired**
Whine	joint parties	Holding something in
dark	Macro view	hand
		Nervous male
hot (object)		Wearing helmet

Tunde Atunrase

CHAPTER 10

The Guernsey Channel Islands Mystery
UFO Case #4

"Everything we see is based on perception not truth. Everything we hear is based on opinion not fact."

The location: **Alderney/ Channel Islands United Kingdom**

Date: **23rd April 2007**

Time: between 2.00pm – 3.00pm approximately

Captain **Ray Bowyer** was flying a routine passenger flight for the civilian airliner, Aurigny Air Services, when he and his passengers gained progressively clearer views of *two* UFOs during a 12 to 15 minute period. Bowyer had 18 years of flying experience, and the 45-minute flight, was one that he had completed every working day for more than 8 years.

Their 80 mile (130 km) journey of 45 minutes, took them from Southampton on the southern coast of England, south-westwards to Alderney, being 10 miles (16 km) from France, and the northernmost of the Channel Islands. Their particular flight path had them converging on *two* enormous, seemingly stationary and identical airborne craft, which emanated brilliant yellow light.[27]

A pilot of a plane near Sark, some 25 miles (40 km) to the south, confirmed the presence, general position and altitude of the first object from the opposite direction. Radar traces also seemed to register the presence of an object, which Ray Bowyer believed to be correlated with the position and time of the sighting.[28]

So here we have multiple witnesses, as well as possible radar confirmation of two very large elongated cigar shaped craft, which the pilot, Captain Ray Bowyer claims he has never seen before in all his years of flying. The story made head line news around the world very quickly at the time.

According to Captain Bowyer;

*"This encounter lasted for fifteen minutes, and the first object being visible from 55 miles distance. On nearing the object, a second identical shape appeared beyond the first. Both objects were of a **flattened** disk shape with a dark area to [their] right. They were brilliant yellow, with light emanating from within, and I estimated them to be up to possibly a **mile across**. I found myself astounded but curious, but at 12 miles distance these objects were becoming uncomfortably large, and I was glad to descend and land the aircraft. Many of my passengers saw the objects, as did the pilots of another aircraft, 25 miles further south"*[29]

Bowyer further added, *"If it was designed by an engineer, that man had to be shaken by the hand because it was a fantastic piece of equipment, if that is what it was. I can't really say much further than to say what I've said all along, that this thing is not from around here"*

Bowyer reported the sighting via the appropriate channels,

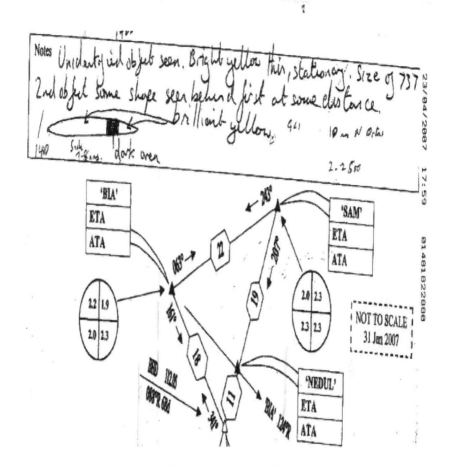

Captain Ray Bowyer's Official Report

"In my case the British Civil Aviation Authority knew within 20 minutes of the sighting, what was seen, as described in a flight log, and faxed directly to the relevant CAA office. The military were informed by Jersey Air Traffic Control at the same time. This is not an option. This is an obligation that crews react in this manner. In my experience, having reported the experience as required has had no negative effect, and there was no problem with me talking about this on British television. Indeed, my company, Aurigny Air Services, have offered every support to [date].

167

The assistance of Jersey Air Traffic Control in releasing recorded information between myself, and the investigating team, has been of great benefit. I did not feel that I was in any danger of being ridiculed, because all I did was to report what actually happened as was my duty as operating air crew"

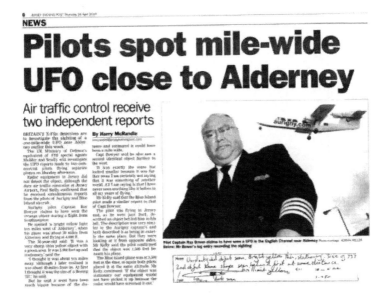

Apart from the two pilots and passengers on board Bowyer's plane there were also ground based reports of the mysterious cylinder type objects over the skies of Alderney.

BBC Radio Guernsey reported that two visitors while on Holiday to Sark enquired at their hotel as to what two bright yellow objects in the sky might be. The objects were observed during an afternoon walk on the 23rd April, in the direction of Alderney. Jersey Airport Radar Control saved a radar recording of the incident, which was submitted to the CAA. These showed traces of two objects with **slow** north and southward movements, for a period of **55 minutes**. They were recorded on Jersey Airport's primary, low level radar system, but not on the secondary radar used for air traffic control, which was screening out stationary objects[30]

As the reader will soon discover, it's important to remember the above statements attributed to the radar recordings in particular the relatively *slow speed* of the objects in question which I believe may shed some light on what these crafts may be.

I decided this would be an ideal case to use remote viewing based on multiple eye witness testimony and supporting ground based observations including official radar confirmation.

The viewer chosen for this particular task was Joe McMoneagle who had been providing excellent information for me on similar cases. I wondered what would Joe make of all this and would we finally identify a genuine extraterrestrial craft or if the reports were to be believed, mile wide mother ships from another world?

Here is the original report in its entirety and Joe's Remote Viewing data complete with sketches:

TARGET: TA60109

Please describe the target, target's origin and purpose of the target.

Description is:

A large disc, which is giving the appearance of being suspended in the air, or is floating very slowly over the ground. Disc is approximately 600 feet across. Disc appears to be partial inflatable and hard-frame bodied, with an inert gas. The exterior of the vehicle is highly reflective from the upper skin, but flat black across the underside. My sense is that this vehicle is completely covered across the top with dark blue sheets of *photovoltaic cells*. These sheets are ultra-thin and completely cover the vehicle's top side. There appears to be at least four drive props which are retractable to reduce wind resistance. [See drawing attached]

Origin is:

The origin appears to be a large flat deck floating in what appears to be a northern sea. Water is salt and very cold. There are a couple small islands visible from about twenty thousand feet altitude, but no other land masses nearby.

Purpose is:

Different forms of long range electronic surveillance.

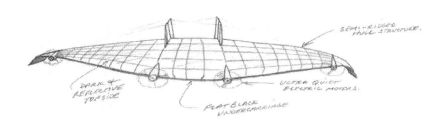

JWM/June 20-29, 2009/1.25 hrs

Once again this was certainly not what I had expected at all and yet it all seemed to make perfect sense. Here we have a remote viewer, being given a completely blind target, who then goes on to describe in full detail, the mechanics of what could only be described as a modern day *Airship,* albeit a rather sophisticated one.

I immediately decided to look up the latest technology based on Joe's rather detailed descriptions not expecting to find much, if anything at all, that would resemble the data but to my surprise I discovered a number of aerospace companies heavily involved in the research and development to some degree of what Joe viewed over the Channel Islands, right down to the use of *'photovoltaic cells'* which I assume could be responsible for the glowing bright yellow light due to the suns reflection off the hull of the craft just as the witnesses reported. I suspect it would also make the object appear as a seamless long or elongated glowing tube from a distance.

It would appear, as Joe expertly describes in his report, that these airborne devices are used primarily for long range Intelligence gathering purposes, and at the time of writing this book, an unverified report was leaked on the internet, and various other media sources of a similar craft of unknown origin, being deployed over the Ukraine border city of Korosten on March 6th, 2014 during the Russian build-up of forces along its shared borders with Ukraine.

Feedback Breakthrough –

Joe's report and description of the unknown object did not match any known airplanes that were being developed at the time but all that would change. On the 6th May 2014, while doing some research for this book, I came across a patent report via an online search based on a few key word searches Joe provided in his data such as *'photovoltaic cells'*, *'Retractable Propellers'* and *'long range electronic surveillance'*

What I found completely floored me as it looked uncannily like McMoneagle's description. Was this the same craft which flew over the Channel Islands? I will let the reader decide for themselves and reach their own conclusions. Note the interesting reference to *'border surveillance'* and the above mentioned Ukraine sightings as an application of the invention. It's also worth mentioning that these devices would probably be more sophisticated today since the original prototypes, which would have been launched or tested between 2006 and 2009. There is also a similar patent for a more delta shape type hybrid airship owned by Boeing based on the exact same technology filled in 2004 and published 2006.[31]

Patent US7137592 B2 - High-aspect ratio hybrid airship - Google Patents

Date of Patent November 21, 2006

The Boeing Company - Chicago

High-aspect ratio hybrid airship
US 7137592 B2
ABSTRACT[32]

In one aspect, a hybrid airship including an outer shell, a plurality of helium filled gas envelopes, and an all-electric propulsion system can have a high-aspect ratio wing shape. In some embodiments, the hybrid airship may be launched using buoyancy lift alone and aerodynamic lift may be provided by the all-electric propulsion system.

In one aspect, *a photovoltaic array* and a high energy density power storage system may be combined to power the propulsion system making the propulsion system regenerative. The high-aspect ratio wing shape provides low drag, and can allow the hybrid airship to fly at an altitude of at least about **100,000 ft**. By continuously recharging the power storage system, the hybrid airship in accordance with some embodiments can stay aloft for months or even years.

The hybrid airship may function as a military intelligence, surveillance, and reconnaissance and communications relay platform.

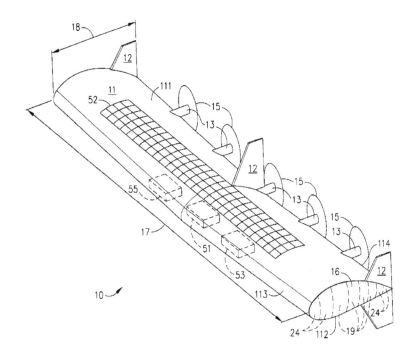

DETAILED DESCRIPTION OF THE INVENTION

The following detailed description is of the best currently contemplated modes of carrying out the invention. The description is not to be taken in a limiting sense, but is made merely for the purpose of illustrating the general principles of the invention, since the scope of the invention is best defined by the appended claims.

Broadly, an embodiment of the present invention may provide an unmanned aerial vehicle that may be capable to operate at very high altitudes for very long flight endurances.

Contrary to the known prior art, the unmanned aerial vehicle of one embodiment of the present invention combines the advantages of heavier-than-air technology and of lighter than-air technology by

174

providing a hybrid airship that may have the shape of a high-aspect ratio flying Wing combined With an all-electric propulsion system. The hybrid airship of one embodiment of the present invention may be used, for example, as a military intelligence, surveillance, and reconnaissance platform, a communications relay platform, and as a platform for directed energy devices. Other applications may include civilian aviation activities, such as reconnaissance and ground surveillance for mapping, traffic monitoring, science, and geological survey, as Well as border surveillance, fishery patrols, or the prevention of smuggling and illegal migration.

In accordance With an aspect of the present invention, a hybrid airship may have the shape of a high-aspect ratio flying Wing. The high-aspect ratio Wing shape may provide low drag, allowing the hybrid airship to fly at an altitude of about 100,000 ft. Contrary to the known prior art, the internal volume of the hybrid airship of one embodiment of the present invention may contain helium only, providing safe operation of the hybrid airship and allowing the airship to be launched using buoyancy lift alone.

Therefore, the need for runways or landing gear can be eliminated by choosing different designs of gas envelopes for holding the helium (e.g., conformal gas envelopes or cylindrical gas envelopes), the buoyancy lift of the hybrid airship can be maximised, or structural efficiency for packaging the helium can be maximised, or an optimal combination of such characteristics can be achieved. Furthermore, by providing the high-aspect ratio Wing With a thick air foil cross-section of one embodiment of the present invention, the hybrid airship of the present invention can be operated at altitudes higher than known prior art aerial vehicles.

Another embodiment of the present invention may provide an all-electric propulsion system for the hybrid airship including low Reynolds number propellers driven by electric motors, a high energy density storage system using either batteries or capacitor banks, and a *photovoltaic array*. Contrary to known prior art propulsion systems, the propulsion system of one embodiment of the present invention may not require fossil fuels or the use of fuel cells. By regenerating the all-electric propulsion system of one embodiment of the present invention by the photovoltaic array, right endurance of the hybrid airship may not be limited by the amount of fuel that can be carried, contrary to the known prior art.

Furthermore, the power output of the electric motors provided in one embodiment of the present invention may be independent of the ambient atmospheric pressure. By providing the all-electric propulsion system of one embodiment of the present invention, the hybrid airship can be operated at very high altitudes for very long flight endurances.

Contrary to the known prior art, the flight time will only be limited by the reliability of the components, which may extend the flight endurance of the hybrid airship of one embodiment of the present invention to one year or more.

Flight endurances this long are not possible using known prior art aerial vehicles.

Still another embodiment of the present invention may provide a method for using the hybrid airship as an unmanned reconnaissance aerial vehicle. By being capable to operate at higher altitudes and for longer flight endurances than known prior art unmanned reconnaissance aerial vehicles, such as the Global Hawk, the hybrid airship of one embodiment of the present invention Will provide break through capabilities in surveillance and reconnaissance.

The hybrid airship of one embodiment of the present invention will be able to operate at very high altitudes out of reach for modern anti-aircraft devices, above the effects of atmospheric Weather systems, and providing a maximized line of-sight radius for sensors and communications equipment.

Due to the long flight endurances, uninterrupted intelligence-gathering, surveillance, reconnaissance, and communications relay missions may be conducted having a higher efficiency than current standard procedures.[33]

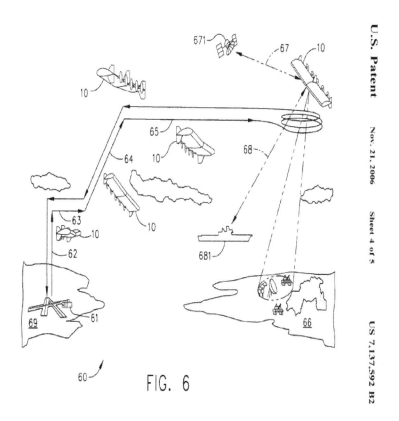

U.S. Patent   Nov. 21, 2006   Sheet 4 of 5   US 7,137,592 B2

FIG. 6

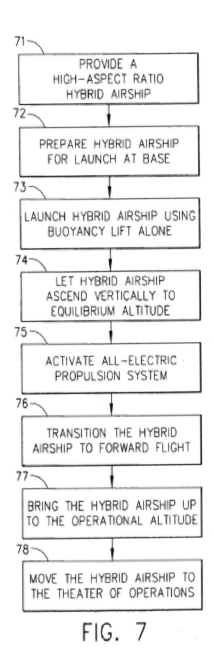

71 — PROVIDE A HIGH-ASPECT RATIO HYBRID AIRSHIP

72 — PREPARE HYBRID AIRSHIP FOR LAUNCH AT BASE

73 — LAUNCH HYBRID AIRSHIP USING BUOYANCY LIFT ALONE

74 — LET HYBRID AIRSHIP ASCEND VERTICALLY TO EQUILIBRIUM ALTITUDE

75 — ACTIVATE ALL-ELECTRIC PROPULSION SYSTEM

76 — TRANSITION THE HYBRID AIRSHIP TO FORWARD FLIGHT

77 — BRING THE HYBRID AIRSHIP UP TO THE OPERATIONAL ALTITUDE

78 — MOVE THE HYBRID AIRSHIP TO THE THEATER OF OPERATIONS

FIG. 7

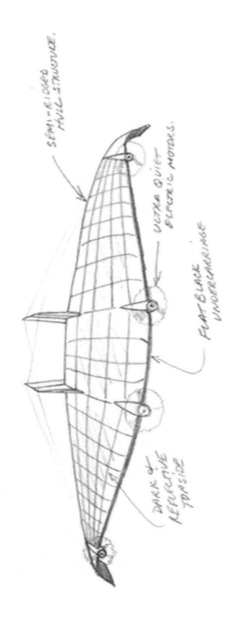

CHAPTER 11
The Rendlesham Forest Incident
UFO Case #5

"We already have the means to travel among the stars. But these technologies are locked up in black projects and it would take an act of God to ever get them out to benefit humanity. Anything you can imagine, we already know how to do"

- Ben R. Rich – Former head of Lockheed Martin's Skunk Works during a speech he gave to the Engineering Alumni Association at university of California In Los Angeles of which Rich was an alumnus. March 23, 1993[34]

Celebrated as the UK's version of the famous Roswell crash of 1947 in New Mexico US, the Rendlesham UFO incident refuses to die down, ever since the public awoke to alarming media revelations of a triangular craft of unknown origin, landing in the forest. What made this case highly unusual compared to other reported UFO sightings was the number of multiple witnesses in the area who all witnessed the event. These were not your ordinary witnesses, but highly trained US military guards, whose sole duty was to protect what was then a NATO frontline defence base for the UK.

On 26th December 1980, American military servicemen, located at RAF Bentwaters and nearby RAF Woodbridge in Suffolk, witnessed a UFO land in the Rendlesham forest which just happens to be situated between the two bases. At first, the men thought it was an aircraft which might have crashed. They followed the direction of the strange eerie lights that had caught their attention.

Two of the men who made contact with the craft and saw it land, Jim Penniston and John Burroughs, both described a small triangular shaped object in a small clearing. Jim Penniston, remarkably, got close enough to touch it! The object was described as metallic in appearance and triangular shaped - either hovering or on legs. It had a set of blue lights on the edges or side and a bright white light on top. Both men watched as the craft took a few minutes to rise and weave past the trees, before shooting off at an impossible speed towards the east and nearby coastline. They also witnessed several other lights, far off into the distance in the same direction. Throughout the encounter, a sense of fear and dread enveloped the entire area.

Detailed sketches of the mysterious object were made and later submitted as evidence for further investigation. The mysterious craft made a return appearance two nights later, on the 28th December 1980. This time, the Deputy Base Commander, Lieutenant Colonel Charles Halt was notified. He gathered a team together and went out in search of the object in the forest.

At first, Halt thought he would be able to debunk the whole affair as some sort of Christmas hoax, but he soon came across the same object again, and realized this was for real. The craft began shooting beams of light towards his men and also directly at specific buildings within RAF Woodbridge. The buildings have been rumoured over the years to be the main weapons storage facility, which at the time, *may* have contained *Nuclear Weapons* according to various sources.

At one point, Halt claimed the object was dripping some sort of molten like substance, which was also backed up by other witnesses who saw not just one, but several objects within the area, in the company of other Military personnel who observed the object. Halt recorded the events on tape and below, is part of the actual recorded transcript of what the men were witnessing:

"I see it too…its back again…

It's coming this way…

There is no doubt about it…

This is weird…

It looks like an eye winking at you…

It almost burns your eyes…

He's coming towards us now…

Now we're observing what appears to be a beam coming down to the ground…One object, still hovering over the Woodbridge base beaming down".

The team witnessed further sightings of other UFOs including how the object appeared to *split* into several parts and shoot off in different directions at incredible speeds, unheard of at the time.

Halt duly reported the events to his superiors and to the MoD in a memorandum on 13th January, 1981. The press soon got hold of the story accompanied by the inevitable avalanche of conspiracy theories which came thick and fast.

The subsequent MoD (Ministry of Defence) investigation, revealed **confirmed** radiation readings at the site of the actual landing of the small triangular craft, which backed up the men's version of what happened that first night and also confirmed the readings peaked where the three holes were located at the site, which incidentally, formed *a perfect equilateral triangle*.

The report indicated the radiation levels were up to *__eight times higher__* than what was expected for that particular area.

I was convinced that this would reveal, at long last, some sort of extraterrestrial data based on the high credibility of witnesses, hard facts concerning the landing site, the Base Commander Charles Halt's own declarations and unwavering belief, that what he and his men witnessed, was of extraterrestrial origin. Plus tape recordings and released official documents, all pointing to the fact that *something* did indeed land in the forest. Something so unusual, so bizarre, it continues to affect all those directly involved to this very day.

The Remote Viewing:

I decided I would focus on only the hard known facts, in particular, **the landing site** and cause of the excessive **radiation** readings that were recorded on that night.

Joe McMoneagle would be needed once more.

The target was set up by his trusted project manager, sealed in an envelope and placed in a pile, along with other targets Joe was scheduled to do. All I had to do was wait till Joe got round to picking my target and do the remote viewing.

I eventually got the results several weeks later via email.

For the first time here is the **only** published remote viewing report in its entirety done by a former U.S. Army intelligence Remote Viewer on the Rendlesham Forest Incident –

[The viewer worked this target DOUBLE BLIND no information was given or shared]

TARGET: TA60308

1. Please describe the target.

2. What is the purpose of the target?

3. ...more questions to follow:

The target is described as follows:

The target location is centered inside a circular road which encompasses an area of what appears to be heavily wooded rolling hills that is approximately 2.5 miles across. This in turn is located within a larger section of woods broken here and there with clearings. The specific target of interest is located in a spot which is slightly on an uphill grade, within a small clearing, due north-northeast of a road intersection. It is close to a long narrow bay area and due west of a much larger lake. The entire area is a wet forest.

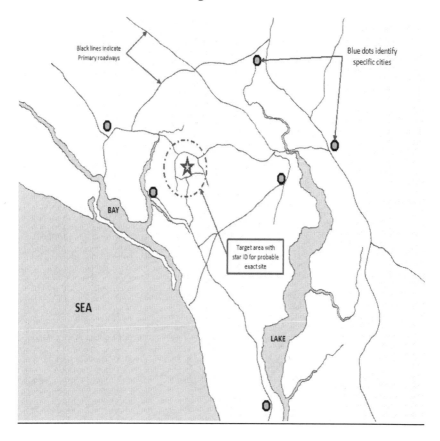

Remote Viewing Sketch of Target Location as drawn by Joe McMoneagle

I get the impression that there is a specific object of interest that falls within this location. This object is described as follows:

a. It is metallic, and roughly shaped like a tall pyramid with three opaque and reflective sides.

b. It is approximately: 6′6″ high; 4′6″ wide [across the bottom edge]; and the same in depth as it is wide.

185

c. The object has legs which are approximately 6′ long that extend from the bottom at three corners; each leg becoming narrower toward the point or ground end. The ground end of each leg is approximately 12″ across and also triangular.

d. The object is vibrating with a very low frequency that is rhythmic and almost inaudible.

e. The object pulses light in the purple, through red, up into the very bright yellow range [in frequency].

This object looks somewhat similar to the following drawings. However; it seems to be constantly changing shapes from/between the representation provided in Fig 2 and Fig 3. This leads me to believe that my perception might be masked by the object which might be either spinning very rapidly, or is somewhat obscured by some kind of a light/force field. Figure four is probably a more accurate drawing of how it actually looks to anyone who is viewing it directly.

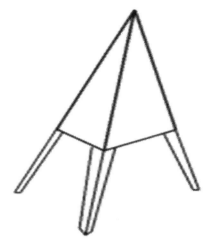

Fig 2.

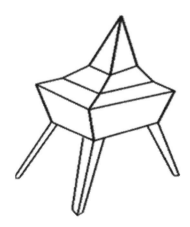

Fig 3.

Fig 4.

Above object is casting what seems like a light blue light underneath where it is hovering; glowing white to light yellow; emitting a very bright white hot yellow light outward for a great distance; and has a slight tinge of reddish colour at the top and bottom as well. The red may be fading in and out.

<u>The purpose of the target is:</u>

My sense is that this is a flight test involving re-entry. This test may have gone badly.

3. Radiation was measured – what is the source?

<u>Radiation source is:</u>

The force field generator is producing the radiation, and it is being emitted from the object in both an outward as well as a downward direction. This is a result of on-board radioactive materials being used in the Force Field Generator [FFG].

4. What is the origin(s) and mission of the object as witnessed by people on site?

Origin(s) and mission of the object as witnessed are:

Object comes from an overhead launch and recovery vehicle which originates from somewhere in the south-western area of the United States. It appears to be a lab facility.

Its mission was to test - launch, evasive flight, and recovery operations under cover of darkness near some other flight facility. If it was perceived while on mission, then subsequent or additional mission essentials were to determine any possible human emotional reactions under duress/stress.

JWM\July 1-6, 2008\RV 2.5 hrs.

I must admit, I was somewhat disappointed and shocked after reading the results. There were no descriptions of ETs whatsoever. The strange triangle, according to Joe's detailed remote viewing data, appears to be a ***top secret unmanned remote controlled craft.*** I was however, *very* surprised by the technology described and its function. I was totally unaware we even had the capacity to produce anything like what Joe came up with. Indeed hard core ufologist's still believe to this day, based on all the data at hand, the paper trail of released classified documents and eye witness accounts, that extraterrestrials MUST be involved in some way.

189

- Had the Bentwaters base personnel been hoodwinked all along? Led to believe what had landed was some otherworldly craft?

- Did the MoD know about this?

- Did the base Commander and Security Commander know in advance what was going to happen that night?

I eventually came across some rather startling information provided by one of the original witnesses, John Burroughs, via an online blog he had set up in anticipation of a reunion between both himself and his fellow Rendlesham comrades. Burroughs made a plea for the other witnesses, in particular, Charles Halt and the base security Commander at the time, Lt Col. Zickler, to come forth and explain whatever it was Burroughs, and the other service men were exposed to all those years ago. The men were now experiencing illnesses they believed was caused by the unknown craft's they encountered up close and touched. It appears Burroughs was seriously questioning the whole ET angle which Halt continues to promote to this day.

Burroughs also queried **Lt Col. Zickler**, who was in command of Security Police and Law Enforcement for the base and squadron at the time. According to Burroughs, Zickler left Bentwaters shortly after the incident and was moved to Eglin Air Force Base Florida, where believe-it-or-not, reports of numerous UFO events soon began to emerge. Zickler then moved on to become Head of System Security Engineering and Chief of Operation Security at GE Aerospace to include *going to extensive lengths to test and create realistic scenarios on an Air Base.*

190

Borroughs then adds a final and rather controversial question which may shed some light on what went on all those years ago,

"Everybody wonders how a Squadron Commander in charge of Security Police and Law Enforcement, can ascend to working with the US Special Forces Counter Intelligence Deception Unit."[35]

Borroughs continues,

"This seems suspicious. Why have you never gone on record about the incident at Bentwaters/Woodbridge?
When I contacted you this week all you could offer was "Cheer up, things will get better soon!"

One of the things that left me scratching my head, was the seemingly advanced level of technology described by the witnesses. If this was a top secret classified military craft, as suggested by Joe's astonishing remote viewing data or part of a psyops/counter intelligence deception operation, which Major Zickler now seems to have extensive experience with according to Burroughs, is there any evidence such technology was around back in the 1980s?

There appears to be some backing for this theory in the form of a host of 1977 patents released online in 2012 by Sacha Christie

Plasma Charged Bolts. http://www.patentgenius.com/patent/4974487.html

Plasma generator. http://www.patentgenius.com/patent/4517495.html

Biofeedback. http://en.wikipedia.org/wiki/Biofeedback

Ion beam. http://www.patentgenius.com/patent/4194139.html

Charged particle beam accelerator
http://www.patentgenius.com/patent/4019088.html

Solid state Doppler radar http://www.patentgenius.com/patent/4160248.html

ELF visual, audio and emotional
stimulation http://www.buergerwelle.de/assets/files/grn/omega16.htm

According to Sacha,

*"THIS WORK WAS SPONSORED BY THE **DEFENSE NUCLEAR AGENCY** UNDER RDT&E RMSS CODE B310080465 B99QAXRA10107 H2590D. ADDITIONAL SPONSORS WERE THE <u>LAW ENFORCEMENT </u>STANDARDS LABORATORY AND THE CONSUMER SCIENCES DIVISION OF THE NATIONAL BUREAU OF STANDARDS,' WASHINGTON,' DC 20234."*

Sacha goes on further to add the following:

*"The events that occurred over that weekend (Bentwaters/Woodbridge) were the actualisation of a joint forces **research project into the behavioural science of staff on nuclear bases.** This exercise involved all three forces and was instigated by the DNA and developed between defence agencies and contractors.*

It was all planned.

Not only was it a behavioural sciences research project but it was also an opportunity for them to field test various very highly advanced technologies. Technology that has left me with my jaw on the floor since 3am Monday morning. The document I found is 244 pages long [36]and I have read it fully three times and parts over and over. I know what happened and have found as many other bits of documentation, including patents to back most of it up, no I haven't selectively chosen to make facts fit, there's just so much of it, I'm overwhelmed."[37]

The reader can access the full report in the referenced links. Is it proof? No. However it does show that the technology was probably available at the time to duplicate most, if not all of what the US Military witnesses saw during that fateful December weekend in

1980 and makes a compelling case that what actually *landed*, may indeed have a more earthly origin than we have been led to believe all these years. On a side note, I did try to find out from Joe more details about the delivery system of the smaller triangular craft and the actual location of the Midwest US laboratory base where he perceived the craft originated from, but he remains tight-lipped (and some might say rightly so), about those questions.

If what Joe describes turns out to be accurate I am afraid the truth of what happened will <u>never</u> be admitted to by either the US or UK governments for all kinds of obvious reasons. After all, you can't openly admit to exposing your own service men or those of your allies and not to mention the general public, to highly radioactive objects?

Indeed I can see why it would be beneficial to promote tales of UFOs, Time Travellers and all kinds of conspiracy and media manipulated agendas to help cover up what really happened. This has always been a well-known tactic deployed by Air Forces round the globe to cover up the existence of highly classified projects.

Nellis Air Force Base and UFOS

Bentwaters was not the first nuclear base to experience an 'invasion' of mysterious *flying triangles*. Similar reports have been noted on US nuclear weapons storage facilities such as Nellis Air Force Nuclear Bomb Depot AREA 2, deep in the Nevada desert not for from Las Vegas. The year was 1998. Once again, another security guard by the name of Christopher Cabrera, while on patrol at the south west perimeter of the base, along with his partner, both witnessed a large flying triangle. The men duly reported the incident and were both summoned to their Flight Chief's Office to give a detailed account of what they experienced. They were told in no uncertain terms to *never* discuss the event and that the incident never happened. They were even threatened with a dishonourable discharge should they reveal what they saw.[38]

Another *military* encounter from 1967

Dr Ardy Sixkiller Clark, a Professor Emeritus at Montana State University reported a similar case to the Bentwaters incident in her book *"Encounters with Star People – Untold stories of American Indians (Anomalist Books 2012)*

Clark published an astonishing story about three former military veterans, all of American Indian decent and their extraordinary encounter with a giant UFO, while on duty at an undisclosed American air force base.

The three witnesses to this event were Arlan, Max and Hank. Dr Clark interviewed all three witnesses and their experiences are summarised below:

- In 1967 an unidentified object appeared on radar. It headed straight for the base and several jet fighters were scrambled to intercept the unknown object. The jets eventually returned to base while the entire base itself was placed under high alert. The men, now wide awake after being woken by sirens, were immediately dispersed around the base perimeters and *ordered* to stay alert.

- The men's squad leader repeatedly told them to keep alert and not to talk. Temperatures that night were close to freezing. The men were ordered to guard the front entrance of the base.

- At 2am the witnesses claimed a 'spacecraft' appeared out of nowhere without making a sound. It hovered over the base for *30 minutes.*

- The object was described as *huge,* 50 to 60 feet wide and 25 to 30 feet tall. Circular in shape with windows. One of the men, Arlan, claimed to see shadows moving, but the light was dull, obscuring any clear vision of the crafts occupants. All the base lights were on, so the men managed to get a clear view of the object. It was metallic, grey, and perfectly smooth with no seams whatsoever. Occasionally the object flashed blue and white lights.

- One of the men on duty suddenly broke rank and ran towards the craft. Max claims he was shooting at the craft despite under orders by their commanding officer not to shoot. He was almost beneath it, when a beam of light from the craft hit him. For a moment, he remained suspended as if frozen, before the beam of light retracted, leaving the guard on the ground. Medics arrived on the scene to take the unconscious man to sick bay *[Max claims he died a few months later due to radiation]*

- The craft then 'moved' and within seconds simply disappeared upwards into the night sky.

- The witnesses were all given 12 hours to prepare for immediate transfers to other bases and never saw each other again.

- They were ordered to never speak of what they saw that night to anyone and were threatened repeatedly. They were eventually informed it was all part of a **top secret test to**

determine how they would react under unusual and stressful situations and that the craft was an experimental one.[39]

I should also point out that like the Rendlesham witnesses, these men also do not believe this was simply a test, yet how does one explain the air of *'expectancy'* and readiness for the appearance of a UFO in this particular case?

Did a similar event occur at Rendlesham? One so shocking it totally convinced the men they were dealing with a real and significant threat from outer space?

There is, as ever, the need to remind readers that until full feedback can be obtained the remote viewing data provided, as detailed as it may be, must remain partially unverifiable till we obtain all the facts. I am simply presenting the raw data and supporting facts about the case for the reader to make their own judgement pending availability of full feedback which may or may never arrive.

There is a lot more to this case that I have left out since the focus was _primarily_ on identifying the object that *landed* and left *radioactive evidence* as observed by multiple eyewitnesses on 26th December 1980. Penniston and some of the other witnesses would later go on to describe debriefing procedures by their superiors and from intelligence agencies such as the Air Force Office of Special Investigations **AFOSI**. Penniston in particular, had 14 such debriefings. *[One wonders if some of those debriefings were carried out by members of the DNA]*

They were subjected to being administered *'truth serums'* such as **sodium pentothal** often used during interrogations, hypnosis and more worryingly – brainwashing!

A similar use of *truth serums* was reported in the tragic UFO case of Edward Bryant as reported by researcher Nick Redfern in his book, *"Close Encounters of the fatal kind."* According to Redfern, Edward Bryant, who passed away at the mere age of 53 from a brain tumour may have been an innocent victim of a covert operation by joint American and UK agencies between 1964 and 1965 to **initiate** and **fabricate** certain "UFO Episodes" in both England and the USA[40]

The reasons for the fabrications noted by Redfern in his book were:

- To determine how successfully the human brain could be scrambled into thinking it had experienced something incredible that actually had no reality to it and...

- To stage-manage faked, mind-managed events to try to figure out how the general populace *[and it would seem Military Personnel guarding highly sensitive locations-Tunde Atunrase's comments*]* might react to **real** encounters with extraterrestrials, should such entities one day appear en masse.[41]

As a result of the truth serum events linked to the Rendlesham case which are a known fact and confirmed by the men themselves, we cannot therefore be surprised that many years later, tales of Time Travellers from Earths future and a mysterious binary code would emerge to muddle the more **factual** and **known** events of that night even further. For a more comprehensive look at the entire affair I would like to recommend, *'Encounter at Rendlesham Forest'* probably the most definitive book on the subject to date and Georgina Bruni's, *'You Can't Tell The People'*.

I have also made Joe's remote viewing data available for John Burroughs and received an acknowledgement from him for which I am grateful for.

On a final note, it is my wish and prayer the men of the 81st Tactical Fighter Wing in Bentwaters who witnessed this extraordinary triangular craft/s in all its glory find some sort of closure to this case and that Joe McMoneagle's amazing report while at best speculative and unverified for now, may help towards giving them vital clues as to what *really* happened in Rendlesham forest all those years ago.

CHAPTER 12
Japan Air Lines flight 1628 incident
UFO Case #6

"It is impossible for any man-made machine to make a sudden appearance in front of a jumbo jet that is flying 910 kilometres per hour and to remain in steady formation paralleling our aircraft. Honestly, we were simply breath-taken."

- Japan Airlines pilot Kenju Terauchi

T he next case and the first to reveal some extraordinary data directly relating to possible extraterrestrial aerial phenomenon and activity, was the amazing tale of Japan Airlines Flight 1628. On 16th November 1986, the flight crew of JAL 1628, a 747 freighter, took off from Paris on its way to Anchorage in Alaska. The crew consisted of Captain Kenju Terauchi, an ex-fighter pilot with more than 10,000 hours flight experience, in the cockpit's left-hand seat; co-pilot Takanori Tamefuji in the right-hand seat; and flight engineer Yoshio Tsukuba.[42]

The routine cargo flight entered Alaska airspace on auto-pilot, on 17th November 1986 cruising at 565 mph (909 km/h) at an altitude of 35,000 ft.

At approximately 5.11pm, all three crew members witnessed two unidentified objects to their left below them. The objects then rose above them and continued to follow their plane. The two objects were described as rectangular 'arrays' of lights grouped together which looked like mini thrusters.

Such was the closeness of the mysterious objects it lit up the aircrafts cabin. The crew could also feel the heat from these objects on their faces.

Eventually the two rectangular objects disappeared from view, but the crew soon encountered another object, much larger in size, which started following the aircraft.

The size of the huge ship was alarming.

Captain Terauchi would claim the size of the 'gigantic' spaceship on his port side was *twice the size of an aircraft carrier.*

The pilots requested an immediate change of course due to the presence of this intimidating and unidentified visitor.

Anchorage Air Traffic Control duly obliged and requested another plane within the vicinity – a United Airlines flight – to confirm the unidentified traffic.

The huge craft however simply followed JAL 1628 in exact formation to any change of direction the captain made which included a 45 degree turn, a decent from 35,000 to 31,000 ft. and a 360 degree turn. There was no escaping this giant leviathan.

Nothing unusual was reported by the United Airlines flight or a Military plane also on the lookout for the reported UFOs.

Captain Terauchi was offered Military assistance by Anchorage Air Traffic Control but the Captain wisely decided against such action.

Eventually the giant UFO departed and the crew eventually lost sight of the craft. JAL 1628 continued on with its flight and arrived safely in Anchorage at 18:20.

Captain Terauchi with Sketch of the UFO

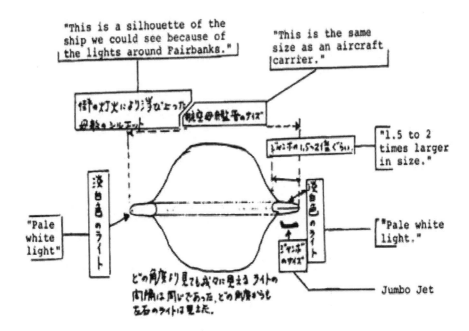

Captain Tarauchi's drawing a month and a half after encounter with a giant UFO

The event made worldwide news. Captain Terauchi in his official report to the FAA and to local media, stood by his story that what he and his crew witnessed were indeed UFOs. It would later cost him his job and a demotion to desk duties. It would be years later till he would be reinstated as a pilot.

The most interesting part of this case which makes it a superior target for Remote Viewing is the availability of radar and official corroborating eyewitness testimony.

The radar information would be a vital clue in support of what happened to JAL 1628.

Remote Viewing UFOS and The Visitors

John Callahan

John Callahan was the Federal Aviation Authorities (FAA) head of Division chief of their Accidents and Investigations branch.

He was initially unaware of the incident when asked to provide answers to the media. He assumed, as most would, that perhaps it was a military test flight or experimental plane such as the stealth bomber. He eventually requested access to the radar data from Alaska to the FAA's Technical Center in Atlantic City New Jersey where he and his superiors played back the entire radar recording's and linked it with the voice tapes by videotaping the concurrent playbacks.[43]

FAA Division Chief John Callahan

A day later at FAA headquarters, they briefed Vice Admiral Donald D. Engen, who watched the whole video of over half an hour, and asked them not to talk to anybody until they were given the OK, and to prepare an encompassing presentation of the data for a group of government officials the next day.

The meeting was attended by representatives of the **FBI, CIA and President Reagan's Scientific Study Team**, among others. Upon completion of the presentation, all present were told that the incident was secret and that their meeting *"never took place"*. [44]

According to Callahan, the CIA officials considered the data to represent the first instance of recorded radar data on a UFO, and they took possession of all the presented data. John Callahan however managed to retain the original video, the pilot's report and the FAA's first report in his office. The forgotten target print-outs of the computer data were also rediscovered, from which all targets can be reproduced that were in the sky at the time.[45]

- So what really happened to Flight JAL 1628?

- What were the strange objects the crew encountered?

- Why was the CIA and FBI particularly interested in the radar data?

I decided to give this target to Joe McMoneagle and see what he would make of it all. I was convinced it would once again, reveal nothing more than some sort of top secret experimental craft which previous RV projects seem to support so far. The only thing I knew for sure and what has been confirmed without a shadow of a doubt, was that *something* extraordinary happened that night and was recorded by credible and multiple official sources.

On the 23rd February 2012, I received an email with Joe's remote viewing data.

The TARGET

The following cue was written on a piece of paper by the project manager without Joe's knowledge, placed and sealed within an opaque envelope with the target ref ID number #12312 and placed in a pool of other mixed targets awaiting Joe's attention.

"What JAL 747 encountered over Alaska, November 17, 1986 at 17:10"

Here for the first time is a full remote viewing session done _double blind_, of what happened as described by the viewer Joe McMoneagle:

TARGET 12312

1. *Describe the target.*

2. *Describe the origins of target.*

Target description is as follows:

Target is a classic UFO approximately 490-500 feet in length, 200-230 feet across in width, and about 55-65 feet in depth or thickness from top to bottom. Object has a mirrored black finish which is capable of changing from an opaque shiny surface with extreme perceptive depth to flat black and near invisibility except for what might be blocked out by virtue of its size. This object is capable of speed in excess of 4,000 mph, but can come to a near complete stand still if needed. The specific speed of the object at the time of targeting is approximately 525-540 mph.

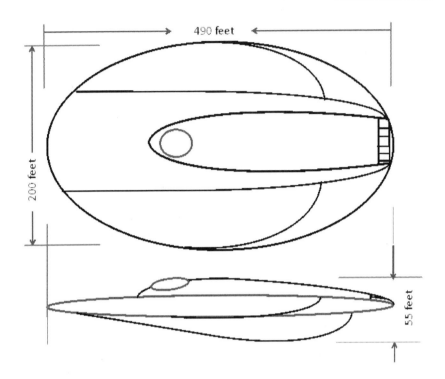

My sense is that at specific time of targeting, it is following another aircraft or man-made object. Engine output is directly aft of the centerline hump, and above the horizontal centerline. Engine output is protected from heat detection, and the entire vehicle is a stealth type of vehicle with the capacity to be invisible to normal radar.

Altitude at time of targeting is approximately 33,000 feet, plus or minus 1,000 feet. Top in altitude is deep space and its low end altitude is 2,000 feet below water surface. Vehicle is capable of extreme manoeuvres and sudden locational shifts and speeds. It can appear to almost disappear and reappear at will.

Power is nearly unlimited, provided it has access to certain minerals and water. A lot of the power deals directly with electromagnetic fields for controlling the power fluctuations and manipulations.

I have a very strong sense that this vehicle is fully automated, and unmanned. I also have a very strong feeling that some other human made airborne craft became involved with a retrieval process initiated by this UFO, and it mistakenly identified the Human vehicle as one of its own, confusing a probe pickup. Erratic behaviour by the human craft confused its procedures for a momentary period of time, but then it successfully completed its scheduled probe pickup and then disappeared by rapidly flying off.

Origins of the target are:

This targeted vehicle is from the following origins:

    a.   The star system provided as follows:

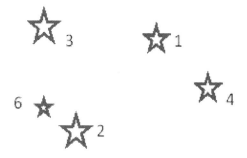

These stars are laid out in the following manner from front to rear; #1-5. The oldest star in this group is #3. The closest star in this group is #1, at approximately 9.7 light years. The farthest star in this group is #6, at approximately 31.4 light years. This star pattern is seen in the north-northeast night sky, and sometimes you are unable to see star #6 as it fades in and out. The star of import within the group is Star #1, the closest star to Sol and Earth.

b. The above ship would be called a *mother ship*. There were two or three other, smaller ships called *vehicular probes*, which were involved in the confusing incident. All three have been seen by the US Military and are known to the US Military and Federal Government.

c. Tasking of this remotely piloted vehicle is **UNKNOWN**.

d. Species responsible for this remotely piloted vehicle are **UNKNOWN**.

e. Name of the specific race or star system this RPV is from is **UNKNOWN**.

The unknowns above are unknown because they reflect from the language or identity of the species that created the RPV(s), and cannot be translated. However, it is my sense that this specific species and craft have been interacting with Planet Earth and other planets within our solar system for nearly fifty years. These RPV(s) are biological-machine interfaces which have been engineered to remain on line for another approximate 50 years before they will self-destruct and/or be replaced by newer models.

RV 1.5 hours\February 23, 2012\JWM

This was shocking news to say the least. Yet, I have come to learn over the years to expect the unexpected when it comes to remote viewing. For the first time, not only was I presented with what could be actual extraterrestrial information relating to a historic UFO event, but also for the first time, I had a possible *location* for its point of origin or wherever it might have come from.

The star map was particularly fascinating and totally unexpected. There was just too much information to process in one simple email and I thought long and hard about the implications of what Joe's data could mean. If the map was correct it would be easy, I assumed, to map the star in question to our known database of nearby catalogued stars.

The only known star that seemed to fit McMoneagle's star chart was the red dwarf, **ROSS 154.**

Ross 154 (V1216 Sgr) is a star in the southern zodiac constellation of Sagittarius. It has an apparent visual magnitude of 10.44, making it much too faint to be seen with the naked eye. At a minimum, viewing Ross 154 requires a telescope with an aperture of 6.5 cm (3 in) under ideal conditions. The distance to this star can be estimated from parallax measurements, which places it at **9.69 *light-years*** (2.97 parsecs) away from Earth. It is the nearest star in the southern constellation Sagittarius, *and one of the nearest stars to the Sun.*[46]

The problem with this star is Joe's data specifically states the star could be seen in the ***north-northeast*** night sky.

I could not find any other stars that fit the range given in the north-north east skies but the reader should be aware that viewers often experience what is known as a mirror effect when remote viewing which might explain the reverse view Joe may have had of the star he perceived. Nonetheless, the distance for the nearest red dwarf does match Joe's data very closely at 9.6 light years. Could **Ross 154** [47] be the same star?

Could there still be another, as yet, unidentified star, within the same range Joe provided?

There has been recent speculation and debate amongst astronomers whether or not red dwarfs could have earth like planets orbiting them or planets capable of supporting life. Joe's data at the very least seems to support this idea which we will explore later on in the book.

The RVPs *(Remotely Piloted Vehicles)* as McMoneagle describes them, are also extremely fascinating; including the propulsion systems and the mechanics behind them, most of which we know are currently being explored in rumoured classified advanced aeronautic 'black projects' involving exotic electromagnetic –anti gravity propulsion technologies for many years.

The retrieval description given by Joe also explains why the UFO Captain Terauchi and his crew encountered, kept following them despite their drastic evasive manoeuvres or change in directions. It would appear JAL 1628 may simply have been in the wrong place at the wrong time and was somehow mistaken by the probe and the 'mothership' for some unknown technical reason.

Having at least identified what the UFOs were from the data at hand, it was time to explore the true UNKNOWNS from the remote viewing session and perhaps maybe even a chance to come face to face with whatever or whomever was in control of these RVPs.

I was not prepared for what followed next....

I sent further questions related to Target 12312 and Joe's Results for further viewing. I finally received the new data on 6th March 2012 via email.

TARGET 12312 (Continued: Part Two)

1. Tasking of this remotely piloted vehicle is?

2. The species responsible for this remotely piloted vehicle are?

3. The name of the specific race or star system this RPV is from is?

Tasking:

There are *three* items these RPV's are here to collect:

a.)   They are collecting specific kinds of genetic material for survival purposes. My sense is that the aliens who have built these RPV's have irreparably damaged many of the gene codes necessary for their survival. They are able to modify and splice genes to the point of living, but not to the point of reproduction. So, as a species they are slowly dying out. Some of our base genes enable us to do things they cannot do; grow larger, stronger, and produce an immunological response against disease that we have never even been exposed to.

They cannot do this.

Through natural reproduction, we are able to replace ourselves with continuing and developing copies that modify and change to meet the challenges we face within our Solar System.

This is something they can't do. They can reproduce, but their offsprings are incapable of surviving for very long because of the significant damage to their gene structures. If they do not intervene in the process and do significant gene modification and splicing, then their offspring are essentially dead or dying within a very short period. To this end, they have sent these RPV's out into the cosmos to find and collect possible genes that could benefit their permanent recovery. So, we are basically providing the raw material they need to survive as a species.

b.)   There are certain materials in the cosmos which are considered to be of great value, even more so than gold; one of them is **water**. Our cosmic neighbourhood is like a desert filled with oases which hold the element called water. Aside for the fact that water is an essential ingredient to life and survival, it is also necessary for the production of energy in how their craft operate and fly. It is especially necessary for entering a gravity environment, and exiting such. Water is an essential to all sentient life forms within the cosmos. It does not matter if the water is fresh or salt in content. In a way, salt is better, because they are able to extract nutrients and other material necessities not usually found in fresh water – kind of a double benefit.

c.)   They are also in need of what are called *Rare Earth Elements* [REEs]. These have a great deal to do with their ability to continue exploration throughout the cosmos. They enable the remotely piloted vehicles to repair themselves, as well as manufacture new cross entity components for exploration, e.g., robots that mimic human or alien interactions with both others [other species], as well as machines necessary to such a mission. Their ships, equipment, machines, entities, and operational systems are all bio-machine interfaces or what we might call intelligent hardware [IH]. This enables them to replicate with some ease of manufacture – do self-repair, re-conditioning, or self-modifications dependent upon the needs within the moment or community. If an inhabited world has an intelligent species existing beneath 2,000 feet of water, then they are able to modify themselves in order to operate at that depth and pressure. If radiation is a problem, or extremes of heat and cold, then they are able to quickly modify and replicate the necessary entities to carry out the mission within the parameters presented. Rare Earth Elements or REEs are necessary to the creation of this bio-mechanical interface, especially when it comes to the wet-wear or bio-software involved.

Specifics of this species are:

This species has long ago learned that travel to distant stars requires something different than personal involvement – it requires a self-replicating, bio-mechanical robotic, operational system capable of intelligent action at least close to that which mimics their own. They also understand that directing and controlling such an exploration system has to be minimalized to the absolute rock bottom least amount of required interaction or necessary direction possible.

Such exploration teams have to be extremely close to replicating themselves as one can possibly be, but not so close that such entities are not expendable on a moment's notice, even to the point of complete eradication of an entire materials collection unit [flight craft, UFO, Carrier, or whatever you want to call it]. Such an explorative bio-machine must be capable of replacing itself from the same matter that makes up the cosmos itself. Such a bio-machine must be designed to learn from its mistakes and to capitalize on what it has learned. In other words, it has to self-replicate and operate as close to what they themselves might want to be or do in any such interaction that might occur between them and any unknown species or entities they might encounter.

So, they are probably close to human in appearance; smaller than we are, lacking in physical stature that we currently aspire to. They are small, thin, friendly, healthy; but somewhat vulnerable, but only when distracted. Their minds are what are most interesting. They long ago discovered that the best means of communication at great distances was through psychic functioning. They have therefore genetically altered their ability to speak, choosing to speak mind to mind rather than physically to each other, as well as to the group in its entirety – what one would call *the group mind*.

This communication is nearly instantaneous without regard to distance, shielding, energy, or time. This communication operates outside what is commonly accepted as the current laws of physics. In reality however, such communications are the norm within the greater cosmic community. Each species has different mind sets which basically insure a kind of light form of encryption from one species to another. In other words, how we feel about apples is an entirely different approach to how they come to enjoy apples. So, the lack of a clear understanding makes things difficult when it comes to mind to mind communications. Once contact has been made, however, a common language of the mind can be established to permit understanding between two species of different origins.

Race name or Star System:

I must reiterate that this targeted vehicle is from the following origins:

a.   The star system provided as follows:

Star Map drawn by Joe McMoneagle

These stars are laid out in the following manner from front to rear; #1-5. The oldest star in this group is #3. The closest star in this group is #1, at approximately 9.7 light years. The farthest star in this

215

group is #6, at approximately 31.4 light years. This star pattern is seen in the north-northeast night sky, and sometimes you are unable to see star #6 as it will sometimes fade in and out. The star of import within the group is Star #1, which is the closest star to our star Sol and our planet Earth. Trying to give this originating species a name is nearly impossible. The same holds true to naming the star grouping or star system, since I cannot make the direct translation from one species to another.

However, I can say that Star One is a Spectral Type M class star, about 1.2 times the size of Sol. It has a mass of approximately 0.8 that of Sol. Average temperature is somewhere around 3100 K. It has a luminosity of about 220,000 and an expected lifetime of approximately 225,000 million years. They are approximately ½ of the way toward the failure of their star. The location of their planet is approximately 0.92% out from their star of the distance Sol is from ours. Most of their planet is also water, occupying approximately 65% of their planet's surface. However, having said this, one could also say that the depth of their oceans does not exceed approximately 12,880 feet at its deepest, with an average depth overall of approximately 650 feet.

They have numerous species on their planet which include flying, crawling, climbing, running, walking and swimming species. There are also millions of species of plants, flowers, and trees on their planet's surface. They are very careful in the management of their planet, having gone through serious problems ¼ million years before. They suffer still from the damage done as a result of runaway use of minerals and fossil fuels in the early portion of their history. They have also suffered from a thousand-plus years of space voyaging; all before moderating what their actions may be.

The numbers of intelligent life forms discovered by their robotic efforts at exploration number in the dozens, but not more than three dozen; actually the number is closer to two dozen than three.

The attached is a copy of what they may in fact look like. Not unlike the robotic representations we are faced by from their exploratory ship.

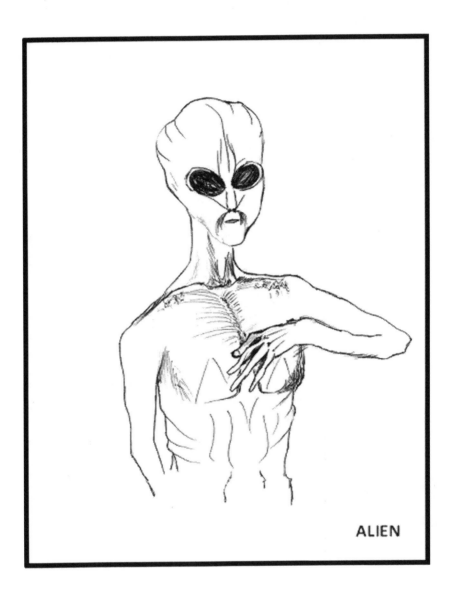

ALIEN

RV\February 28th – March 4th\ 2 hrs\JWM

Remote Viewing UFOS and The Visitors

As you can see from Joe's comprehensive report, he feels we are dealing with an extraterrestrial race, relatively near to us in light years terms. They have been visiting us for many years and need our resources for their own survival. Much of it reads like a sci-fi report yet this is precisely what many witnesses to ET activities have repeated over the years. The big bug eyed beings with large heads and small frames acting in robotic fashion cold and unsympathetic in some cases only communicating via telepathy to their victims or experiencers as some call themselves.

It's hard to accept all this may be true and yet - our governments seem not to be aware, interested or acknowledge such a thing may be going on in our world today, or so the general public are led to believe.

How does one for example explain the treatment of Captain Terauchi by the media after witnessing such a remarkable event? Why the continued ridicule and systematic debunking of others who have encountered similar experiences over the years?

If what Joe says turns out to be true, and we have no way of knowing for sure until we come face to face with these beings and identify their home world, then there is no way elements of our Governments and leaders do not already know about these extraterrestrial visits. In fact I do not know what would be worse - That our leaders simply turn a blind eye to the 'possibilities' of what Joe and many others have described or the confirmed existence of a global cover up of such knowledge from the citizens of Earth for decades.

Either way, it makes no sense at all and begs the question why would such information be withheld from the public?

If the CIA, FBI and President Reagan's Scientific Study Team were fully aware of the radar reports of JAL 1628's encounter with a giant *"mothership"* and as the FAA's own John Callahan claimed considered the data to represent the first instance of recorded radar data on a UFO, then why all the secrecy? By the way I seriously doubt this was the first time such craft were recorded on radar but it is still an impressive case if not one of the best recorded UFO cases due to the overwhelming evidence at hand now partially supported by professional remote viewing of the highest standard.

The Aliens described by Joe remain unverified at this time but I can't help but notice the possible parallels between their reported current dilemma and where we are as a species today. How ironic it would be if indeed our oceans and water which we often take for granted, could in fact be the only real cosmic currency of note.

Perhaps once we finally realize this simple truth maybe we might start taking care of our planet before we reach the point of no return. Sadly, I fear that line may have already been crossed several times over. One only has to look at the terrifying future that lies ahead for our oceans due to manmade disasters such as the catastrophic ongoing nuclear disaster in Fukushima, Japan.

I hope, if anything, Joe's mindboggling report will inspire debate and further investigation over the years as we continue to await feedback and full Government disclosure regarding extraterrestrial visitations. I also hope it helps our never-ending quest and understanding of humanity's place in the cosmos and the role of consciousness, psychic functioning or telepathy as a valid communication and information gathering tool of the future that may help bring the world of *The Visitors* much closer to ours.

Remote Viewing UFOS and The Visitors

CHAPTER 13
The Travis Walton Mystery
UFO Case#7

O ur final case would be the most extraordinary remote viewing session I have ever come across, despite the lack of feedback available to verify some of the data that was produced. The target this time, which as it turned out, would be the last target in search of ET craft and their origins I would undertake. It involved an in-depth look into one of the most celebrated alleged UFO Alien Abduction cases ever recorded in modern history.

I was somewhat skeptical about this case from the very beginning for a number of reasons, but in the end, what finally made me take a chance on the Walton case, was the simple fact no one else, as far as I knew, had attempted this target or published any remote viewing data on the events that had been reported. I decided to give it a go, if nothing turned up or if it turned out to be just another hoax, at least we might find out one way or another.

The Event
On Wednesday November 5th 1975, Travis Walton, Mike Rogers, Steve Pierce, John Goulette, Kenneth Peterson, Dwayne Smith and Allen Dallis, seven loggers all working on a tree thinning contract in the Arizona Apache Sigreaves National Forest USA, had finished working for the day and began making their way home to Snowflake that evening in their old 1965 International pick-up truck. It was around 6.10pm, while driving along the quiet road

through the forests, the men noticed an eerie glow behind the trees in the distance, some 100 yards ahead. Travis Walton, then only 22 at the time, thought it might have been fires set off by hunters or headlights. As the men continued to drive closer to the scene of the mysterious light, they suddenly came face to face with the unexpected. Right there in a clearing amongst the trees was a classic UFO hovering above the ground amongst the trees.

The men could not believe what they were seeing.

"It's a Flying Saucer" cried out Dallis.

Travis wanted a better view and had already got out of the truck to get a closer look at the object. The craft gave off a soft yellow golden colour, illuminating the surround crest area. It appeared to be 15 to 20 feet in length and no more than 10 feet high. It remained silent and totally still – suspended in mid-air.

Travis began to approach the craft, while the rest of the terrified men, paralysed with fear, remained in the car and yelled at Travis to get back. By now, Travis was approximately 6 feet beneath the object – The men continued to cry out to Travis to get back into the truck.

Suddenly-- and without warning, the mysterious craft made a strange mechanical noise and then began wobbling followed by a burst of a beam of light, a foot wide, which hit Travis directly on the chest, throwing him some 20 feet away onto the ground. His body appeared lifeless, or so his fellow loggers thought. The men shouted and made a hasty getaway from the terrifying scene they had just witnessed, occasionally looking back, to check the object had not been following them.

Eventually they stopped and realized they had to go back for Travis. They speculated as to what might have happened to him - had he hit the ground alive? "No, he was in one piece", claimed Steve, while Dwayne said he heard a zap as if Travis had somehow *'touched'* a live wire.[48]

After a brief but heated debate, they decided to turn around and go back and get their stricken co-worker.

However, once the men arrived at the site, Travis was nowhere to be found. They searched everywhere, calling out his name but could find no trace. Nothing, it was as if Travis had simply *vanished* into thin air.

Time was running out. They had to notify the authorities of what happened. They headed back to Heber, Arizona and informed the local Deputy Sheriff Chuck Ellison, who at first, did not believe them, but upon seeing just how terrified and upset the men were, he began to take their claims seriously.

A search operation began that morning, involving officials and volunteers around the scene of the abduction, but nothing was ever found. By Saturday, the police were now using helicopters, horse-mounted officers and jeeps. Travis Walton had disappeared off the face of the earth – Literally.

Shortly afterwards, word of Walton's disappearance became worldwide news.

Two days later, on the 10th November, the loggers were subjected to stringent polygraph tests performed by Cy Gilson, an Arizona department of Public Safety employee. All of them passed their examinations except for Dallis, who did not finish his test which invalidated his results. Below is a quote from Gilson's official report:

"These polygraph examinations prove that these five men did see some object they believed to be a UFO, and that Travis Walton was not injured or murdered by any of these men on that Wednesday".

"If the UFO was fake, five of these men had no prior knowledge of it".

Following the polygraph tests, Sheriff Martin Gillespie announced that he accepted the UFO story, saying **"There's no doubt they're telling the truth."**

Travis was finally found traumatized, but otherwise safe and well in a phone booth, after making a frantic call to his brother from an EXXON Gas station near Heber, Snowflake -

He had been missing for 5 days!

From what Travis could recall, he remembers being hit and subsequently knocked out by a beam of light from the UFO. By the time he came round, he found himself awake on board a space ship. He claims he encountered several small 'Alien' beings looking over him, in what appeared to be an operating room. Terrified, He managed to escape these beings temporarily; walking briefly within the halls of what he assumed at the time was some kind of hospital, before stumbling on what looked like a large room with a chair in the middle. Travis sat in the chair and noticed the controls on the chair acted as some sort of *directional guidance systems* – he could also see stars all around him, which only came into view once he moved closer to the chair and sat on it.

He discovered if he moved away from the chair, back to the main door of the room he entered, the viewing screen or area showing the stars would disappear showing just a wall.

Then the terrifying truth dawned on him....he was on board a *spaceship*. It's unclear whether this was the same 'spaceship' that had hit him with the beam of light.

Just as he began to panic, a *blond haired* man appeared in the doorway, wearing a *blue skin-tight suit*. Travis was relieved and thought someone from the Military or Police had come to rescue him. The *blond being* didn't say a word and ushered Travis to follow him.

He was led out of the craft into what looked like a huge hanger. Travis has speculated this hanger may indeed have been a much larger ship. He saw several other silver shaped oval objects inside the hanger similar in size to the one that had fired a beam towards him.

He kept asking the *blond man* questions but he remained silent; while firmly, but gently, directed Travis into another room where he met three other *Humans*, two men and a woman.

Humans?

These *humans* appeared to look just like any other human, they all had blond hair, were physically fit and muscular. Except for their unusual eyes – *there was something about them Travis could not quite identify* - and an uncanny "*family resemblance*". Apart from that, they all looked perfectly human. They never spoke a word to him and proceeded to lay him on some sort of medical table, before placing a contraption over his mouth which made him lose all consciousness. The next thing Travis remembers is waking up on the highway in the dark and watching a huge silver metallic object hover above him before shooting off silently at an amazing speed.

As expected, Walton's re-emergence 5 days later caused a sensation. He underwent medical examinations and a polygraph test. In the meantime, skeptics and debunkers claimed it was all a hoax, but the authorities were satisfied with the results of the polygraphs, thus ending one of the world's most fascinating tales of alien abduction to date.

- *So what really happened on that fateful day on the 5th November 1974?*

- *Did the event occur as claimed by 7 sworn witnesses, or was it just another hoax?*

- *What happened to Travis Walton during the 5 days he went missing?*

- *Where did he go?*

- *Who or what were the strange beings he encountered? Where they a figment of his imagination? Was he hallucinating?*

- *If the UFO was indeed real, where did it come from?*

- *Why was it here in the first place?*

These were just some of the questions I, and I would imagine, many others fascinated with this case, have been dying to know. If this was a single eye witness account usually I would not go anywhere near it with RV, but due to the high number of eye witnesses to the initial encounter it made perfect sense to start there and try and establish if their story would be corroborated via remote viewing, done under a double blind protocol and by a proven remote viewer of the highest order.

Once again Joe McMoneagle would be the viewer of choice for this project. I knew if this was a hoax he would quickly unravel such a plot and gather the necessary information required about the target.

As I mentioned earlier, I was highly skeptical we would find anything of note, due to the high level or false leads we had already unravelled including misidentifications and out right hoaxes in previous remote viewing projects. Would this case prove any different?

We were about to find out.

I contacted Joe's company and discussed the target with the project manager, who as usual, made certain the highest level of blindness was adhered to at all times, ensuring Joe had no access to the questions behind the target or any other related information whatsoever.

The following target cue was set up and written on a piece of paper, placed within an opaque envelope and sealed; left in a large pile of existing targets Joe would eventually get round to doing.

Here, published for the first time, is a full remote viewing session done <u>double blind</u> of what happened as described by remote viewer Joe McMoneagle:

228

TARGET 62912

[Target question sealed within an Envelope]

"What happened on November 5, 1975 to Travis Walton?

(dob: 2/10/53)"

TARGET 62912

1. *Please describe the target.*

2. *What are the target's primary intentions?*

Target described as follows:

There are what appear to be two targets present.

Target One:

Initial perception of this target is a very **bright light**. This is then followed by a perception of two flat discs – with a flat side and a bulbous side. The flat sides of these discs are pushed right up against one another in a way that seems to produce an extraordinary amount of energy. Both discs are approximately five feet off the ground and seem to be hovering, or possibly are being supported by something difficult to see. The following can be said about the target object [See **drawing A** below]:

1. *They are exceptionally hard.*

2. *Metallic to the touch. This metal finish is an alloy with a thin coating of some other kind of metal.*

229

3. *There is a very bright light aura surrounding the two discs.*

4. *There is heat associated with this aura as well. It is hot enough to give you a severe burn trauma.*

5. *Object is approximately 35-40 feet in diameter.*

6. *There is nothing live aboard the object.*

7. *There is a slight humming noise coming from the object.*

8. *There are hollow parts to the object.*

9. *The object finish is almost like a mirror.*

Object is sitting in a clearing within woods, just off of what looks like a logging trail, and there is one human associated with this target.

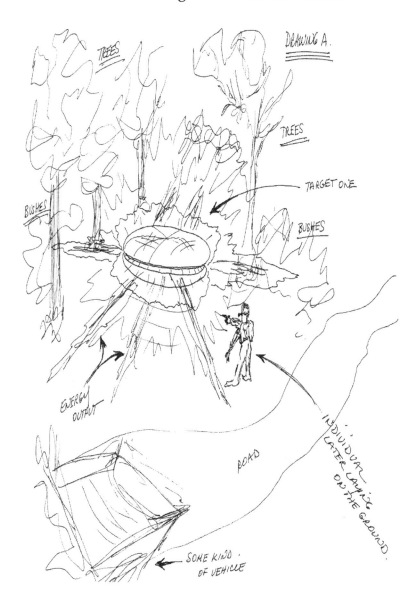

Drawing A

231

Target Two:

My impressions of target two is that it differs completely from target one. Target two is irregular in shape and a very dull color mixture which is kind of bleeding all together. The target has panels or segments which open outward on heavy hinges. Where they have these panels, I have a sense that it is right behind the power section or where a drive motor is located. There are also clear panels which you can see through. My sense is that these are made of glass. There is a large open flat segment of this target that is attached to the drive section of this target. The following can be said about this object [See **drawing B**]:

1. *Target two is smaller than target one by half.*

2. *I get a sense that there are humans associated with this target object, perhaps as many as four, or possibly two I see standing away to the side.*

3. *I get a strong sense of panic among the humans, like they are running away from something.*

4. *People are moving from object perceived as target one to target two, and then getting inside of target two.*

5. *Target two is quickly moving away from target one*

6. *One of the people is somehow on but not inside of target two and he falls off.*

7. *Target one continues to pulse and glow. My sense is that this was an accidental encounter.*

8. *It is possible the one person who fell off of target two might be injured because my sense tells me he is prone and not moving.*

9. *Target two leaves the area, leaving one person on the ground. This person appears to be injured with a possible head injury. My sense is that they've abandoned this person to whatever may happen.*

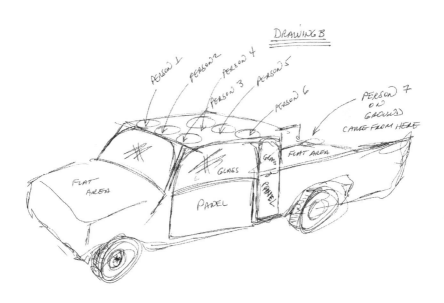

Drawing B

233

Question Two:

What are targets intentions?

My sense is that this is a scout vehicle which is unmanned. It is here to take samples of soil, air, water, and whatever else it can collect. My sense is that this is the intentions of target one above. Target two above is a different object which was located very close to target one. This specific target apparently isn't intelligent enough to have intentions, other than to do what people tell it to do – so this is some kind of a robotic vehicle manipulated by humans – possibly a vehicle, probably a ¾ ton pickup truck.

There is a distinct and strong possibility that this object referred to as Target One is possibly a *multidimensional object*. I say possibly, because it occupies a different place in space than where it sits as targeted. My sense is that this is a very *dangerous* object while it is operating within our space/time threshold.

JWM/July 26, 2012/2 hrs 15 minutes RV time.

Remarkably, Joe's data seems to corroborate the events witnessed by the loggers with minor discrepancies. We know that Travis didn't fall off the truck but willingly left the truck of his own accord and approached the object on foot, walking almost directly under it according to his own testimony and those of the other men who watched him at the scene.

234

We at least can now confirm Joe was on target and I needed him to elaborate further on the data he had acquired without giving him any clues as to what the target is. **Remember all the information he is providing at this point is produced without him knowing what the target is.**

Further tasking will be based solely on whatever data Joe provides.

The following cue was given to Joe to elaborate on his previous data several weeks later by the project manager:

TARGET 62912-B

"Describe your impressions for this time period - The next five days post the original target date"

Description is as follows:

One of the human forms present at the event site apparently has fallen backward from either an automobile or a truck, or possibly a platform of some kind. It is my perception that it was probably a vehicle of some kind, because it suddenly began moving at great speed.

When he fell, he struck his head quite violently on the ground. The concussive force was not very great however, as it is my sense that this was an area of open dirt or ground, that is possibly covered by moss or detritus collected over time from dead leaves and smaller tree limbs that have begun to rot or decay. It is the whipping action that slammed his head backward that probably did most of the damage.

The extent of his head injuries was sufficient to have created swelling of the brain tissue within the cranial cavity - although this would not have happened immediately. I believe he struck with enough force to be knocked unconscious for at least a period of five to ten minutes.

While regaining consciousness, he found himself alone with whatever the object is that is putting out the very bright energy field. My sense is that he was completely abandoned by his buddies.

I see him moving back toward the object in order to see if there might be someone within the object that could help him. His head at this time would be giving him considerable pain, and he is probably dizzy and suffering from a lack of balance. I believe he actually touched the object more than one time, and each time he touched it, he received a major jolt of electrical energy emanating from the object itself. This on top of the fall and striking his head would have done sufficient injury that he would have no full memory of much of this interaction.

My sense is that this object is designed to drive people and animals away, while at the same time jolting them with enough energy that they would have no interest or intent in pursuing a continuing contact with it.

Suffering from this damage to his mental capacities, and having the swelling now impacting on his actions and/or ability to think and act, he cannot remember which direction he arrived at the event scene from, nor would he be able to remember why he was there, who he was, etc. Suffering so, it is my belief that he wandered off into the woods trying to get away from the object, lights, and general activity going on in that area.

At some point, realizing they had left their friend at the event site, they would have managed to turn the vehicle [possibly a truck or a car] around and begun to return to the event site to retrieve their friend. My sense is that when they did eventually arrive at the site, what they found was the object had departed, or was in the process of departing. I get a sense that they are looking kind of up and off in a singular direction – as the remnants of the light fades off in the distance passing through the upper limbs of the trees until out of sight.

It is fully dark now; they have very little light, and what they do have is from a couple of flashlights and perhaps headlights from their vehicle. They are in a panic and scouring the ground looking for their friend and calling out his name.

Their friend meanwhile has wondered completely away from the event site, and has moved deeper into the woods. Even if he was capable of hearing them, I'm not sure he would have because of the head trauma he suffered initially. He is now nauseous, has a massive headache, and feels very sleepy because of the brain swelling. All he wants to do is lie down in a soft place within the woods and sleep. Which he eventually does, never acknowledging the now soft and distant calls from his friends. It is my perception that it is getting colder and damp, and his friends rationalize that their friend has probably been taken from the area by the strange floating light they witnessed earlier. Because of this assumption, they decide to withdraw and report their experiences to the local sheriff.

The Sheriff has a lot of difficulty understanding exactly what it is that they are reporting. Each of them has a completely different experience from the event, and they all have equal difficulty in explaining it to them or anyone else. My perception is that the local Sheriff responds as he would with any possible event of a like nature - he calls out all of his militia to look for the missing man. They go back to the general area of the event, and scour it over and over again with bright beam lights and dogs. This produces nothing at all because their friend has awakened, and in a near coma-like stupor continues to wander further and further from the search area. After twenty-four hours and no results at all, they cancel the search and return to their homes, with the idea that perhaps his friends have either murdered him themselves, or something has happened which no one can account for. Of course in the mind of the Sheriff, the probability is for the prior.

I can almost see what happens over the next few days. All of the missing man's friends and neighbors are brought in one at a time and they are interrogated. The Sheriff tries to determine who had the most anger or the best reason for killing the missing man. Who was the one who set the event up and why? I suspect that the Sheriff had no ability to come up with any evidence at all in this regard, because the event was real and most likely a full contact with a UFO vehicle.

I can sense that as the days pass, the missing man becomes healthier. The swelling in his brain goes down sufficiently for him to regain his senses, but he can't put the event together in his mind because of **all the missing pieces**. I get a sense that eventually he comes upon a building of some kind and is able to contact someone by using a phone. They simply drive out and pick him up. He now appears to be suffering from very little trauma, having recovered most of his mental faculties, and evidence of his head damage being pretty much mitigated by time.

Of course he is suffering from a mild case of amnesia, severe dehydration, and has missed enough meals to have lost considerable weight. Sleeping in the wild, not completely understanding what happened to him, and having segments of memory of the UFO experience probably gave him nightmares for quite some time afterwards.

This entire episode I sense transpired over a period of perhaps four or five days. It's difficult to tell because when I try and get into the mind of the missing man, it becomes quite confusing and complicated. My sense is that he really was suffering from a severe brain trauma and damage to his memory, both short and long term.

Remote Viewing UFOS and The Visitors

RV/1.5 hours/August 15-20th, 2012/JWM

I was complete floored by the level of data Joe had come up with. Joe's exceptional remote viewing skills describe most of what we already know about the men's encounter with the object as backed up by sworn polygraph testimony. Quite remarkable when we consider once again Joe has absolutely no idea what the actual target is and no information was provided up front.

However, the biggest revelation I found was the *possibility* Travis may have been wandering around alone, suffering severe brain trauma. This begs the question if he was out there alone, how come the entire search team failed to locate Travis for *five days?* I understand the search effort was not extensive for the first couple of days which we know angered the seven loggers and their families a great deal, prompting the Sherriff to call out helicopters and additional militia to help in the search effort, yet even this failed to locate any sign of Travis, not even a trail.

Could they simply have missed him? It is a possibility, and probably the most logical explanation. However, if this is indeed the case how do we then account for Travis's recollections of events which seem to be very clear and as far as we know he has not changed his story since the news of the abduction first broke.

Joe's remote viewing report, sensational as it was, and full of new and intriguing information, seemed to bring up even more questions.

For now, I would just have to accept the data for what it is, just another piece of information (partially unverified) to add to the mystery.

I wanted to repeat the successful efforts of the JAL 1628 project and see if we could use remote viewing to trace the *origins* of this mysterious object with the following key questions:

- *Where did the craft come from?*

- *What was it?*

- *What were the propulsion system and technologies used in this craft?*

- *Who was responsible for sending it out there and for what purpose?*

So far there was no hint of a hoax described in Joe's data in relation to the actual craft itself, but in my mind, there was always the possibility we were we dealing with another Rendlesham incident.

It was becoming clear more work was needed on this case; however, little did I know just where this would all lead to. I was totally unprepared for what came up next.

Joe was given the next tasking based only on his *own* data produced in his previous work. He remains completely blind to the original tasking and has been provided no other information other than what he has produced himself, while working completely alone as required by the remote viewing protocol.

TARGET 62912 – CONTINUED:

A. *What is the origin, beginning point of travel, from which this object you described comes?*

B. *Describe how it got from there to here.*

Origin – beginning point of travel is:

This place is called by many names, but is primarily known as **"The Dog Star,"** officially **"Sirius,"** which is the brightest star in our night sky. It is also known as Canicula [Latin for Little Dog], Aschere, Alpha Canis Majoris, Sothis [name given by the Egyptian astrologers of ancient times], HR 2491, and HD 48915. This star is probably the most important star in the sky to most of the ancient world's cultures, as many of those cultures talk of men who travelled from this star and/or its companion, which is not visible to the naked eye.

I get the impression that all of this "object's interest" circles the companion to *Alpha Canis Majoris*, so what's going on has something to do with the dwarf star, *Bravo Canis Majoris*. Where Canis Mojoris lies has everything to do with why we are having contact with entities from that star place.

Sirius is approximately 6.5 light years from planet Earth. It is one of the closest stars to us. My perception is that there are probably seven planetoids currently circling the star. Of these, at least three are inhabitable from an Earth-like viewpoint. These have blends of breathable gasses which we could survive breathing, although our atmosphere has a slight variation which is different. This difference has to do with mostly with helium and another inert gas.

What led me to this constellation was the impression of a dog chasing a hunter through the woods. At first I concentrated on the hunter, but that didn't seem to be where the information was centered. So, I switched to the dog and got an impression of unconditional love, or commitment to life.

This seemed to be an appropriate line of understanding. My sense is there is an intelligent life form that originates from this star system and they have a major interest in all other inhabitable stars within reach of their own for some mysterious reason.

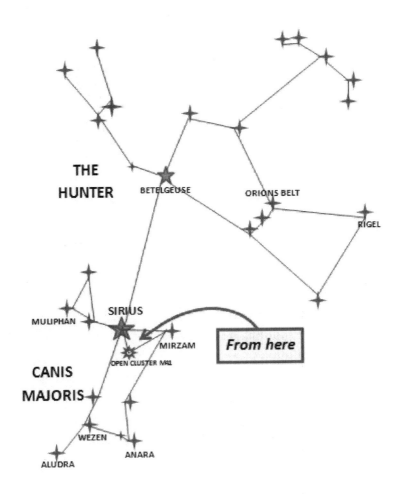

Star Map drawn by Joe McMoneagle

This leaves me with some other rather interesting perceptions; such as why? Why would any entity want to make any kind of contact with us? So, I asked this question and got fed back to what I was originally drawn to in the first place – the unconditional love of a dog. That and the fact that we are not the only ones they are apparently concerned about. This is about what's good for a much larger group and not specifically aimed at individuals.

I get the impression that we are not the only intelligent beings between here and Sirius Alpha. I keep getting an impression of a very large envelope surrounding the Sirius star locale and within this very large envelope we, as well as dozens if not hundreds, of other intelligent species current exist. Some of these entities are well ahead of us, and of course some are behind us in terms of development. Within this envelope are millions of stars, the majority of which are uninhabitable.

My perception of this envelope, expanding outward like a perfectly round ball or perhaps a balloon, is that it is probably not a good thing. Or, at best it is a good thing and a bad thing simultaneously. I suspect the more advanced intelligent species out there understand perfectly what is going on and this is a good thing too. They understand, hence why this particular view is a good view of what's going on.

The good thing issue has to do with changes to DNA, some of the most rudimentary forms of DNA. So, it has something to do with the spread of a kind of radiation that alters DNA. Much or even most of the DNA is altered to the point of being sterilized completely. So, this is kind of like the way we preserve food or sterilize things like those we use in hospitals at present. When food is cooked and stored, or when an object is sealed in plastic for later use within a surgical suite, we usually sterilize it by passing it through a major source of Gamma Rays. I get the sense that this is what's probably going to happen. Some DNA, which exists as very rudimentary animal life in the deepest pits and oceans of water across the universe will be enveloped by Gamma rays and this small dose that reaches the bottoms of these very deep rifts will be just enough to alter the DNA of primitive life forms so they begin to grow and change in some way that eventually produces a form of life that is intelligent. This is probably how we started, how our own species began at some point in the dawn of existence.

The down side is that this same wave or massive discharge of Gamma rays will completely sterilize DNA that is openly exposed to the burst thereby ending whatever life that might represent. In other words, all the intelligent life on planets for as far as that envelope will reach will cease to exist within a very short time after being enveloped. So, that which starts life also ends it.

When will this happen? Probably not for a very long time in Earth years, but within time itself, or measured by the lifetime of planets, it is just around the block – a half million or million years perhaps.

Sirius is a binary star, and as such, it has a very small dwarf twin (Sirius B) which is about the same size as that of our Earth. It has been bleeding off into Sirius major for a very long time, and as it has done so, the gravity of this star has been growing in major doses. Eventually, this smaller dwarf twin will collapse to the point that it becomes unstable and goes nova. The sudden collapse and explosion of this small star will be sudden and horrific to life as we know it within range of the expanding ball of Gamma Rays it will produce. As that wall of Gamma rays passes through the Earth, and it will, because Sirius is only 6.5 light years away; all life as we

244

know it on this planet will cease. This is the driving reason for these entities reaching out to our planet for seemingly mysterious reasons. They are either collecting DNA samples for further seeding on other similar planets, or they are setting the stage for full contact in order to save what they can.

How it got here:

My sense is that this is a probe. It is not manned, or if it appears to be manned, it is manned by clones specifically bred and then released after some internalized training to do a certain kind of job. When they are finished, which only takes days, they self-destruct by walking into the machine that disposes of their corporal bodies. That which is captured or collected by this probe is properly stored within shielded segments of the ship and returned to Sirius with the probe.

The way it got here is by opening a singularity within time/space. It does this by generating a massive amount of power at a very small point in space/time. Once this tiny hole has been opened, it uses the material which bleeds out of the hole to produce more energy. Since, the material is passing out of the very crucible that is capable of building reality itself, this amount of power is enormous – almost beyond our capacity to understand. There is a massive reaction to this effort, which creates a backlash within space/time reality that has the appearance of a wave. The probe sits at the leading edge of this wave, enabling the wave itself to envelope it. The wave doesn't move however. What it does is pull the backside of space/time to the front/side of space time, kind of like folding a sheet of paper end to end. As this occurs, the probe appears to leave here and appear elsewhere; that elsewhere being the Sirius system itself. They do not travel through space/time; they bend it to suit themselves. The probe doesn't travel from there to here space itself twists and turns, traveling around the probe eventually bringing there here.

This takes an enormous amount of power and energy, which comes directly out of the ability to create time/space. There is no need to control its production, since how it's used is 100% efficient to do what is necessary.

Note:

It is very difficult to work on a target which cannot be verified in any direct or objective way. These are difficult targets as historically they are personally exhausting. It's almost as though I have to reach a long way to get the information in many cases. In short, I have to almost fight the exhaustive need for sleep in order to complete them. So, there is something debilitating about these kinds of targets, but I can't explain that either. Just remember these are very difficult, and almost impossible to objectively evaluate.

JWM/RV 1.5 hours/September 26-27, 2012.

It took me several days to process just what I had read and even then, it sounded too unbelievable. Yet, was it really that far-fetched? I spoke to a few astronomers about the possibility of Sirius B going supernova any time soon without mentioning where I got the idea from; they all seemed to concur that it was not beyond the realm of possibility for the star to go *Nova* within 500 – 1 million years.

It brought home just how *vulnerable* we are on earth as a species and why we should be looking towards the stars for the continuation of the human race. We cannot stay here forever seems to be the primary message I was getting from Joe's report.

I was blown away with the technology described and left wondering if we will ever be able to prove or duplicate such manipulation of time and space on the scale Joe described.

There would be lots to ponder and think about as time goes on but for now I will leave that up to the experts to debate the merits and possibilities of what can only be described for want of a better word, or rather concept....*Time Travel*.

As extraordinary as Joe's report was, there was something still missing. Something that had somehow slipped by, unmentioned throughout the entire project.

Who actually sent the craft?

Travis claimed he saw two types of beings; a small statured alien type, with large menacing eyes (See his book Fire In The Sky for a full description)[49] and of course, the famous *Humans*. It's important to note, Travis does not refer to the humans as aliens, even though they appeared to have *strange eyes* and a *familiarity* between the ones he encountered. There is also the possibility the blow to his head and subsequent brain trauma, may have completely altered his perception or memory recall of what happened. That part only Travis can answer and we have no real feedback to go on besides taking his word for it. *[There have been numerous cases similar to Travis's encounter, where the abductees or those who have had close encounters with human looking aliens, have had unexplained memory loss, as if their minds were wiped – Usually in these cases, the persons memory gradually returns but often leading to great stress and mental confusion for the victims]*

However, there is the possibility he may have experienced something of a *multidimensional* nature. After all, if we recall, Joe did say he had a hard time trying to get inside Travis's mind due to all the confusion going on in his head at the time, which may or may not have been a deliberate attempt by an advanced race to shield Travis from the trauma of his encounter with an extraterrestrial vehicle. There is the possibility Travis may have been interacting with whoever was controlling the vehicle. His body -- or a percentage of it – may have bi-located and remained in the forest.

Missing time appears to be a common theme for those who experience close encounters with unearthly objects. A well-known case very similar to Travis Walton's was recorded back in 1977, just two years after the Arizona encounter.

Carlos Valdes, a Chilean soldier, was in shock after a weird, *five-day* ordeal with a UFO. Six members of an army patrol saw two bright objects descending from the sky. Valdes, the patrol leader, set out alone to investigate and, according to the men, simply *vanished*. Fifteen minutes later, they said he reappeared, tried to speak and passed out. The date on his watch had been advanced *five days*, and he now had about *a week's growth of beard*.

The uncanny similarities with Travis's own five day disappearance are striking and seem to suggest the possibility Travis may have been picked up, taken away for 5 days and returned back to the same *place* and *time* he was originally taken. Remember Travis himself was shocked to discover he had been missing for so long.

Could this be further evidence of advanced alien craft operating as *time machines*?

In any case, we still needed to find out who was ultimately responsible for the craft Joe had viewed. Remember Joe still does not know what the original target is all about and his RV journey so far, has taken him literally *light years* beyond the original target site. Could he tell us more about the civilization responsible for such an advanced piece of exotic hardware?

CHAPTER 14

THE SIRIUS MYSTERY

"I believe that these extraterrestrial vehicles and their crews are visiting this planet from other planets which obviously are a little more technically advanced than we are here on Earth."

-   **Colonel L. Gordon Cooper**
    (Mercury 9, Gemini-5 Astronaut)

We now had RV information, (unverified I might add) of a point of origin for the UFO encountered by Travis and his crew. We also have an idea and several possibilities of how it got here and why. What we don't know is who was responsible for it.

Please bear in mind Joe still has no idea what the target is and he is only going on what he has produced so far. We decided to give him the next challenge and see what he could come up with this time.

For this Target it was decided by the project manager to create a new Target ID. Published here for the first time, is the complete remote viewing session done <u>double blind</u> by remote viewer Joe McMoneagle:

250

Remote Viewing UFOS and The Visitors

Target 12913:

[Target sealed within an Envelope]
**"The most intelligent beings from the <u>Sirius Star System</u>
currently interacting with Earth beings"**

Question: Please describe target

TARGET 12913

Describe the Target within the envelope.

<u>Description of the target is:</u>

I'm getting a description of a human figure which is very much like what one would imagine a Viking to look like; very Nordic, perhaps originating from the extreme north of Sweden, Norway, or maybe even the Finland area. I get the impression that this is a very old or ancient culture that goes back many years from today.

If I were asked about the differences that I might notice between the males and females in this race of people, I'd have to say that it is almost non-existent. This leaves me with an impression of a more *androgynous* race of people. If it were not for light colored facial hair on the males, it would be difficult to distinguish between them as to their sex. This is a beautiful race.

They average rather small in stature, something between five feet and five feet three inches in height; between 140 pounds and 170 at the heaviest. The females are not that much different in either height or weight from the males – both having very strong muscular features, with very little body fat. They have powerful hands and wrists, and are very well developed across the chest

251

area. Their hair is a very light brown to very blond, almost white in some cases, especially with the females. Both male and female wear their hair very long and loose; sometimes restricting their hair at the forehead with a small band that looks metallic. This metallic band may in fact denote rank or stature amongst them.

Their cheek bones are very high and their faces are somewhat angular. They have flat foreheads that angle back in a more pleasing way; thick and sensual lips; their nose is somewhat smaller than one would expect for the kind of facial characteristics; and their ears are small, well-formed and close to their head. Their eyes are angled upward toward the outside, with a slight curl at the inside corner, reminiscent of the Asian fold but not quite. They have very large irises that are very light in color, like very light blue sky to very faint green. Some have eyes that have a slight red or pink tint to them as well. The iris is interesting, in that it is slightly oval top to bottom, and if it were more so, they would have cat like expressions – intelligent but a slight hint of fierceness to them. Their skin is pink to cream in color, with some rosiness to specific areas exposed to weather. They are prone to burn if exposed to too much Sun light.

My sense is that these are not very gentle people, but have the ability to deal with threats easily and with much speed and whatever strength may be necessary for survival. I get the impression, that much like Vikings, they travel far across oceans of dark seas, and do not fear going where most have not been before. They are very courageous and have an ability to survive however tested. They could be good friends, but equally a difficult enemy.

252

very
androgynous.

Original Remote Viewing Sketch by Joe McMoneagle

©Tunde Atunrase 2015

TARGET 12913 [Continued]

Follow up Questions:

1. *Please describe home world, in detail, including its location, structures, and technology advancement; like in transportation, etc.*

2. *Is this a physical being or from some other dimension?*

<u>**Questions Continued:**</u>

1. <u>Describe the home world – as follows:</u>

The world is very much like Earth, except they have only about half the water Earth supports. The planet is a little bit smaller and lighter than Earth, and is one of *12 other planets* circling their star. The Star system is known formally by us, as **Alpha Centauri – B**. The specific planet we are talking about is the third planet of the 12, and circles the star at about 156 million kilometers radius. It is the third planet out from the Sun, and this planet has *three moons*; one approximately half the size of ours which is in a fairly rapid and erratic orbit, and two others approximately half the size of the first which are of equal size to one another. The two smaller moons have very stable orbits which are perhaps half the distance from their planet as is our moon. Temperatures are also stable on this planet and run between -19 and +36 degrees Celsius. The planet has really bad storms. These storms can sometimes rage for as long as a week at a time. They are fairly stationary and very destructive to above ground facilities. My sense is that most of the people of this planet probably live underground, and live very comfortably. They are approximately 750 – 1,000 years older than our race and subscribe to a traditional culture quite similar to ours – e.g., they like and appreciate music, art, medicine, etc. As for their abilities with technology advancement such as transportation, these things are impossible to describe, because I lack the knowledge to explain any of it.

2. <u>Is this a being which is physical or other dimensional:</u>

These are physical beings, but they are also beings capable of understanding multidimensional aspects to space travel. In other words they are capable of bending time/space to serve them; not only in transportation, but in many other things, such as food production and in the manufacturing of many other products. These beings are just too far ahead for me to understand most of what you are asking.

RV 1.5 hours/April 10-15/JWM *(2013)*

This was mind blowing stuff. I was not sure what to make of it all. Joe describes another humanoid species living within the Alpha Centauri Star system. If we take the remote viewing data at face value, despite the lack of feedback at this stage of the project, this particular race of beings have mastered the secrets of Interstellar space travel; seemingly being able to move from the Sirius star systems to their home world/s of the Centauri system. For all we know, they may even have colonized star systems all across the galaxy and perhaps maybe even to other galaxies?

I think it's also important to note the fact that Joe not only validated that a genuine UFO was involved in Walton's case, and while he suggests Travis was wandering the forest for days, it seems oddly coincidental that Walton describes being on a genuine UFO with humanoid blond people. Yet here we are with Joe describing blond humanoids connected with a UFO originating from Sirius, which also turns out to be the place of origin of the UFO Travis and his co-workers encountered that fateful night. If Joe's data turns out to be correct the implications are enormous.

Of course this is all speculation until we gain feedback on the subject; however Joe's data is highly specific in describing things we know we should be able to get feedback on such as the identification of planets within the Alpha Centauri systems.

It turns out we may not have long to wait for some of the data described by Joe to be verified to some degree.

In 2008, the scientific community was rocked by the announcement and possible discovery of *a planet* orbiting Alpha Centauri B.

*"Alpha Centauri Bb, as astronomers have named it, is a possible extrasolar planet orbiting the K-type main-sequence star Alpha Centauri B, located **4.37 light-years from Earth** in the southern constellation of Centaurus. If verified, it would be the closest extrasolar planet to Earth ever discovered, and the lowest-minimum-mass planet detected so far around a solar-type star. Its existence was announced in October 2012 by a team of European observers, and the finding received widespread media attention. However, the announcement was met with scepticism by some astronomers, who believed that the European team was over-interpreting its data".[50]*

"Starting in February 2008, and continuing through July 2011, a team of European astronomers, mainly from the Observatory of Geneva and from the Centre for Astrophysics of the University of Porto, recorded measurements of Alpha Centauri B's radial velocity with European

Southern Observatory's HARPS echelle spectrograph at the La Silla Observatory in Chile.

The team made 459 observations of Alpha Centauri B's colour spectrum over a four-year period, then used statistical filters to remove known sources of variance.

On 16 October 2012, the team announced they had detected an Earth-mass planet in orbit around Alpha Centauri B. *The discovery was presented in the scientific journal Nature, with lead author credit going to Xavier Dumusque, a graduate student at the University of Porto. He called his findings "a major step towards the detection of a **twin Earth** in the immediate vicinity of the Sun".[51]*

"Alpha Centauri Bb was discovered using Doppler spectroscopy. As it orbits Alpha Centauri B, its gravity causes extremely small (semi-amplitude of about 0.5 m/s) periodic shifts in the host star's velocity. Variations of the line-of-sight velocity component cause tiny shifts in the star's spectrum. Using an extremely sensitive spectrometer, the team was able to infer variations of 0.51 m/s in Alpha Centauri B's radial velocity. The ESO called the findings the most precise measurements ever recorded using the technique. The team estimated the probability of a spurious detection at 0.02%."[52]

"On June 10, 2013, scientists reported that the earlier claims of an Earth-like exoplanet orbiting Alpha Centauri B may not be supported. The existence of the planet remains a subject of scientific debate, and research by at least three separate groups of astronomers is ongoing"[53]

Possible additional planets in the Alpha Centauri system

Further astonishing information lending support to Joe's data regarding the number of planets within the system, was highlighted within the latest Wikipedia report below:

*"Astronomers have already ruled out the existence of Neptune-sized planets or larger in the Alpha Centauri system. However, because of its proximity, stability and lower mass than the Sun's, **astronomers believe that Alpha Centauri B is one of the best possible candidates for the detection of an Earth-like planet by Doppler spectroscopy.** Statistical analysis of results from NASA's Kepler Mission indicates that low-mass planets tend to form as members of multi-planet systems, **so the discovery of Alpha Centauri Bb means that it is likely that there are additional low-mass planets in orbit around Alpha Centauri B.***

*These hypothetical companions are likely to have wider orbits, and would be difficult to find with current instruments. The HARPS spectrometer can only detect changes in radial velocity of about 30 centimetres per second, whereas Earth's gravitational influence on the radial velocity of the Sun is a mere 9 centimetres per second. An astronomer in the Alpha Centauri system looking toward the Sun with this equipment could not find Earth. **Detecting additional planets in the system will become easier when the ESO's next-generation spectrometer ESPRESSO comes online in 2017.** ESPRESSO is specifically designed to look for Earth-like planets, and will provide radial-velocity measurements several times more precise than those used to find Alpha Centauri Bb.*

Of particular interest are planets within the habitable zone of Alpha Centauri B, estimated to lie between 0.5 and 0.9 AU. In 2009, computer simulations showed that planets were most likely to form toward the inner edge of that zone. Special assumptions are required to obtain an accretion-friendly environment farther from the star. For example, if Alpha Centauri A and B initially formed with a wider separation and later moved closer to each other, as might be possible if they formed in a dense star cluster, the region favourable to planet formation might extend farther."[54]

According to astronomers, we should be able to detect additional planets within Alpha Centauri B around 2017.

Remote Viewing UFOS and The Visitors

Would remote viewing aide in their efforts in finding these planets? Would astronomers be brave enough to trust the data Joe has provided and indeed, has provided in similar operational circumstances for his government so well over the years? I would like to think so, but such is the attitude towards psychic research of any kind, let alone one involved in the search for alien worlds, that I doubt it would be taken seriously, which is a shame, but at least the data is now out there. Even amongst remote viewers within the so called 'elite' RV community there is a negative attitude towards using remote viewing for cosmic exploration, esoteric or UFO targets.

Their fear is that such associations do the science of remote viewing much harm, drives potential clients away, and will attract UFO and doomsday zealots into the community. This has been an issue lately on various online forums, YouTube channels, Facebook sites and numerous radio outlets and as demonstrated in this book the lack of feedback and the complete disregard for proper remote viewing protocol can lead to disaster which is the primary reason for the problems these targets have created for the RV community in the past.

What is needed is proper awareness, education and guidance on how to tackle targets like these in an acceptable, ethical manner, rather than avoid them altogether or turning ones nose up at any target that has insufficient feedback. I have learned a lot from Joe and Ingo's approach to RV and greatly admire their courage to step forward and share their vast wisdom on how to tackle targets such as these. Remote Viewing schools can learn a lot from Mcmoneagle and Swann's work in this particular field of RV rather than worry about the kind of people RV attracts while at the same time, being more than happy to take students money and fail to teach them the fundamental basic protocols of remote viewing. Thankfully there are still some credible RV instructors around who are trying to address the situation.

There are scientific mysteries out there that require good honest, experienced and talented remote viewers and remote viewing project managers to engage in, just as much as the pursuit for money, lost treasure or missing people. We are curious creatures by nature and should never stop exploring, even when we don't have all the answers just yet.

All we can do is hope other open minded cosmologist, scientists and astronomers will at least give Joe's locations and data for this mysterious planet some serious thought.

On a more positive note, should or rather *when* astronomers finally verify the existence of multiple planets within the Centauri system, I hope it will be verification of the work Joe has done and who knows? It may, one day, eventually pave the way for serious research into using remote viewing to locate and identify habitable planets of other nearby star systems.

The Nordics and other Humanoid species visiting Earth:

"Extra-terrestrials that resemble human beings should have evolved on at least some of the many Earth-like planets that have been discovered by astronomers"

Professor Simon Conway Morris

University of Cambridge

Assuming for one moment the remote viewing data from Joe McMoneagle turns out to be correct concerning the existence of these Nordic-Type humanoid beings from the Sirius and Alpha Centauri star systems, is there any evidence such beings have been visiting the earth on a regular basis?

Not surprisingly hard evidence is lacking on that front, however, if one begins to take into account the numerous eye witness testimonies as far back as biblical times and even some of Earths oldest cultures and mythologies, there does appear to be a significant and vast amount of information which does not rule out such a possibility. For example, could the mythical Nordic Norse gods actually be extraterrestrials visiting earth? The Norse cosmology is interesting in that respect with references to Super beings with magical weapons of mass destruction, originating from *nine* home worlds inhabited by life forms often described as giants and elves amongst other things.

More recently, we have tales of contact between humans and what has been described as human looking aliens who have managed to blend into our culture virtually indistinguishable from

Earth humans. This was the era of the *Space Brothers* Contactee movement; Individuals who claimed to be in contact with humanoid extraterrestrials visiting earth. At the height of the early Contactee movement, various names such as George Adamski, Daniel Fry and Howard Menger to name a few, all claimed to have met human looking aliens. However, another contactee probably not as well-known as the above, yet equally controversial, was a South African woman named Elizabeth Klarer.

Klarer claimed to have been in contact with beings from Alpha Centauri from 1954 to 1963 and according to her autobiography, *'Beyond The Light Barrier'*, she also claims to have been taken to one of the planets in the Centauri system for several months and then returned back to earth. She describes her stay on the planet in detail, as well as the very *human looking* aliens and their lifestyle.

It's impossible to verify Klarer's story of course, and it is only mentioned in context with the possibility of an alien species residing in the Centauri System. Other famous contactees who claim to have met humanoids from Alpha Centauri include Sixto Paz Wells; a well-known UFO researcher from Peru, and author of the book, *The Invitation* and his sister, Veronica Paz Wells, author of the book, *The Sowers of Life*.

Both books describe human looking extraterrestrials living mainly *underground* on not just planets within the Alpha Centauri system, but also within our *own* solar system. Alien bases have been described underground on Ganymede, one of the moons of Jupiter and the largest moon in our system, as well as underground bases here on Earth, Mars and other planets.

As a side note, I once took part in Remote Viewing project done way back in July, 2004 which featured looking at some rather unusual structures on the planet Mars. I was one of *twenty four remote viewers* scattered all around the world who had absolutely no contact with each other during viewing or being given any information about the target. It was all done completely blind.

The Target Coordinates and cue was:

MLF4 –WJ84

*Describe whatever is **underneath** the area marked for focus in the feedback photograph.*

Gave a re-tasking, T5UV74, 25July04-08:47AMCDT:

Describe PURPOSE/FUNCTION/REASON for "visual anomalies" in feedback

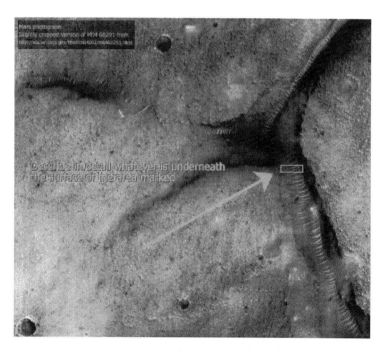

It was a fascinating project, which featured so many corroborating bits of data from the viewers who took part. It was also one of the most bizarre sessions I had ever done, because I had no frame of reference to properly decode what I was getting, apart from the fact I felt I was *somewhere remote*, desolate and a long way from home. At least I thought I was, till I started picking up *humans* for some reason and rather attractive ones at that. I remember at the time thinking this was crazy and seriously thought about removing one particular sketch from my session which made no sense at all, with regards to the other data I had got. In the end I decided to leave the controversial sketch in the final session and submit what I got. Its only today, 10 years later after seeing Joe describe Human looking aliens living mostly underground somewhere in Alpha Centauri did I remember that old sketch of *a woman* (at least I thought it was a woman), staring right at me, from a target related to something unknown, *underneath* the surface of Mars!

Could there be intelligent life beneath the Martian surface? I have my own thoughts on the subject, but for now, I'm happy to just wait and see what we will eventually discover out there once the shackles of secrecy are removed completely concerning life on other planets within our solar system, as well as full disclosure on any 'possible' classified international covert space programs the general public may not be privy to at this time.

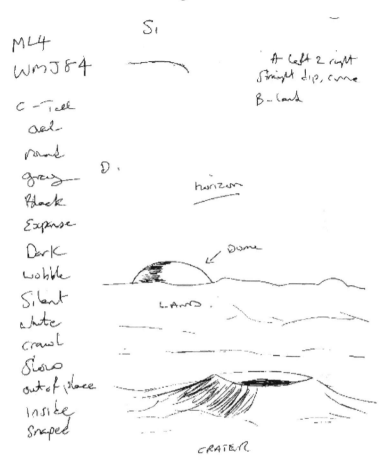

ML4

WMJ84

S1

A Left 2 right
Straight dip, curve

B — land

C — Tell
cal
road
grey
Black
Expanse
Dark
wobble
Silent
white
crawl
Slow
out of place
inside
Shaped

D.

horizon

Dome

LAND.

CRATER

[The reader can check out a YouTube clip trailer of The Mars Anomaly project and additional information on how to access all the data pertaining to this target at the following link http://www.dojopsi.com/rvexpo/Mars/]

Until Joe's data arrived, I have often wondered why there are so many reports of underground alien bases. It appears - and this is just my own hypothesis, that perhaps apart from secrecy reasons, in order to remain hidden from view, maybe these civilizations are more aware of the need to *protect* themselves from the harsh realities of the cosmos and have long understood that for a species

265

to survive over a long period, long term surface dwelling may not be such a smart move. Consider also the growing negative effects of radiation from various types of Stars. There is also no way to escape sudden cataclysmic and unpredictable cosmic disasters, of which there are many, including as we read earlier, the ultra-devastating effects of a *Supernova* or any number of extreme climate change scenarios.

It appears some governments on Earth, may already be shifting their focus to going underground. Could this be one way of restoring ecological balance to the planet and allowing the earth to regenerate, rather than continue to use up valuable natural resources due to over population, deforestation, pollution and war? We may not even have a choice in the matter as I see it, if we are to survive beyond the next several centuries. Underground cities and artificial domes, (with advanced climate control systems) may be our only way forward as well as seeking out new worlds to colonize to ensure the continuity of our species.

Only time will tell.

CHAPTER 15

Joe McMoneagle and Ingo Swann's views on Remote Viewing Extraterrestrials

So what do the two giants of remote viewing Ingo Swann and Joseph McMoneagle have to say about ETs as it relates to Remote Viewing in general? Ingo has written one book on the subject of extraterrestrials where he revealed his own spectacular real-life encounters with what he claimed was a humanoid alien back in the 70's in Los Angeles.

In *"Penetration: The Question of Extraterrestrial and Human Telepathy"*, Ingo Swann Books, 1998, Ingo addresses the issues of how to communicate with an advanced alien intelligence, and the role of telepathy as a primary or universal form of communication. More controversially, he addresses the possibility of an advanced form of telepathic influence possessed by such advanced races we may not be aware of, and the implications of this if they are to be proven to exist.

Ingo also described how he was approached by a shadowy government agency to remote view what turned out to be according to Ingo, extraterrestrial structures and machinery in operation at specific locations on *the Moon!* Of course none of this has been verified within "official circles" however there has always been rumours of cover-ups and conspiracies surrounding the moon which continue to this day.

Ingo also claims to have remote viewed the surface of Mars in a private RV project several years ago and appears to support McMoneagle's claims as well as so many other remote viewers including myself the 'possible' existence of extraterrestrial structures above and below the surface of Mars.

Ingo leaves us however with the same note of caution I have repeated throughout this book, that for remote viewing to be done successfully, there must be feedback with which to evaluate accuracy. Until then, "whether a remote viewing has occurred" is pending the time when feedback is forthcoming.

Joseph McMoneagle has been more forthcoming regarding his own views on the subject and has actively taken part in several UFO conferences to demonstrate the pros and cons of remote viewing anomalous targets of extraterrestrial origin.

Joe remains, as far as I know, the only former ex-military remote viewer to have been tasked by his government on one specific UFO incident which he reveals in his book *Mind Trek.* He received confirmatory feedback of the target once he was summoned to the Pentagon after he indirectly filed for official access to the classified photo of the UFO. His request immediately raised eyebrows and after some time he was eventually shown classified photos of the object he had been tasked against, but not allowed to take them. What did Joe make of the UFO itself?

"In my own mind, there is no doubt as to these objects authenticity. Its presence at a target was as real as any other element I could have described. Was it really there? I, as well as my client, believe that it was"

For a full description of the craft and actual sketch I recommend readers to check out McMoneagle's book, *Mind Trek – Exploring*

*Consciousness, Time, and Space Through REMOTE VIEWING –
Hampton Roads 1993.*

Over the years and during the course of writing this book, I have
gathered quite a bit of information regarding Joe's thoughts, beliefs
and predictions concerning the existence of The Visitors; where they
come from, how to locate them, how they communicate, when
contact will eventually be established and how they manage to
travel such vast distances across the cosmos.

Here is a summary of Joe's findings to date:

- Joe believes extraterrestrial craft operate outside of our
  current known laws surrounding time and space. These
  beings are aware of how to manipulate these laws and have
  discovered a way to manipulate time and space, allowing
  for near instantaneous travel from one location to another
  and do not require the need to enter real space and time to
  reach their destination.

- As a direct result, extraterrestrials can travel into the future.

- Another by-product of their ability to warp space and time
  and operate outside its boundaries is they can use this for
  communications.

- Psychic Functioning or Remote Viewing, is another form of
  communication which operates outside the boundaries of
  time and space.

- All humans possess some level of psychic ability and as a
  result, we are being *unconsciously* manipulated to a certain
  extent.

- Our species development may be tied to extraterrestrial development and vice versa.

- Intuition and creativity can be downloaded, or passed down to us from extraterrestrials, as long as we are open and willing to use it.

- Our desire to enter and explore space – our accelerated intelligence and the growing knowledge that we are not alone in the universe, is part of an overall plan, which all intelligence may be subjected to.

- The more intelligent species arise within the universe, the faster our development will accelerate – Those who come before, eventually aid or assist in the development of those who follow.

- ETs are using a form of sub-quantum emissions for communicating instantaneously across space and time.

- Our intelligence and consciousness is being automatically altered at the DNA level and we cannot alter or prevent the process.

- Some ETs are bi-pedal, with upper arms and multiple finger-like appendages. Their brains are not unlike ours, only more developed. They breathe a form of atmosphere which is similar to ours. They bear live children, like most mammals, they have eyes like ours, but see in a different frequency band. They speak and communicate as we do. They have humour.

- All our previous and current contacts are with drones designed and engineered for deep space missions. True aliens are not like those we currently deal with.

- There are at least **three different species** that are already collecting materials and samples from our planet. They are aware of each other and where the others are from.

- When they decide to make contact, it will be both pleasant, as well as unpleasant. We won't be harmed, but contact will be on their terms and not ours.

- There are certain long established and well entrenched laws regarding interstellar entities and how we will be required to act.

We will have no choice in the matter

- Alien life is very similar to ours because of the similarity of our DNA.

- Aliens are carbon-based entities very similar to ours - but due to unique differences in our physical worlds, they will probably not look *exactly* like us.

- Heavier gravity, flooded or dry worlds, extreme climates, and survival necessities, may give them advantages when compared to us.

- They have the same passions, wants desires, and necessities we have, and possess a like interest in spirituality.

- Contact probably will not take place until around 2075.[55] At the moment Joe believes we are currently dealing with their drones.

Finally Joe believes the reasons and delays for full open contact are because ETs are waiting for:-

- The end of human tribalism.

- Human reproduction to peak.

- For us to mature as a species.

- Our sincere desire for peaceful contact and

- Our need to understand more.

[All Comments courtesy of Joe McMoneagle 2011]

CHAPTER 16

Where do we go from here?

"Unknown objects are operating under intelligent control... It is imperative that we learn where UFOs come from and what their purpose is. I can tell you, behind the scenes, high ranking military officers are soberly concerned about the UFOs"

-Admiral Roscoe Hillenkoetter

(Former director of the **Central Intelligence Agency**)

What does it all mean for those of us still looking for further answers to *The Visitors* and their continued interest in Earth? If we accept the various professional remote viewing reports presented here, done under the tightest of scientific protocol allowed and taking into account, certain elements of the targets that are yet to be verified with feedback, we have to accept the possibility there may be some truth to what we have uncovered so far, pending further availability of full and accurate feedback. This raises profound and highly significant implications not just for ufology or Remote Viewing, but our entire species as a whole.

When we finally acknowledge the reality of extraterrestrial life and discover that the humanoid blueprint, is *not* exclusive to just our planet alone, it could potentially revolutionise every aspect of our society. From religion to finance, *nothing* would be the same again. Indeed, such a race of beings, looking very similar to humans, could potentially be walking among us and we wouldn't even be aware of their presence.

I have no doubt it will be an uphill struggle at first to get the message across to everyone and for the subject to be taken seriously, but once we eventually overcome that hurdle - which I believe won't be far off, the world *might* benefit immensely from such revelations, at least that is the hope and the prayer. The reality though, is we must equally be prepared to be wary of those 'other' advanced and less advanced civilizations out there, that possible might not have earth's best interest at heart and as a result, we must do everything within our *own* power to step up our efforts to openly embrace all areas of research into the extraterrestrial phenomenon in a truthful manner. Decades of unchecked denials, cover-ups, disinformation and debunking will not aide in making whatever decision our so called 'leaders' on the issue at hand may make any easier, and could in fact, lead to catastrophic unforeseen consequences if the **wrong** alliance or decision is made without 'open' consultations with individuals and groups within our best academic and scientific institutions around the world, who have humanities best interest at heart.

Also, those who prefer to sit back and pretend this will all fade away like a bad dream, are just as guilty as the true believers who feel ETs will come and rescue mankind. The truth is we need to embrace difficult questions, challenge ourselves to solve our own problems and accept there is an awful lot we just don't know about any of this stuff. We need to be more open to studies in consciousness, get back to basics, put our egos aside, and accept the reality of ESP and its possible role or links in relation to other alien species who may be thousands, if not millions of years ahead of us.

Failure to do this, could lead to trouble in the years ahead for reasons that should be obvious to the reader by now.

I was asked the question the other day well if *The Visitors* are already here and have been, by the looks of it, for eons, then how come they don't make their presence known more openly? Why don't they just land in front of well-known iconic locations such as Buckingham Palace, The White House, the Vatican during Sunday Mass, interrupt special televised events while the world is watching such as the Super Bowl, or similar major sports events witnessed by billions around the world at the same time?

I can only assume their reasons for *not* landing so openly is because we are not ready to accept their reality, preferring instead to make contact with selective individuals of their own choice, who may be open to their advances, but who sadly often end up being the butt of jokes, ridicule and systematic orchestrated debunking, whenever they go public with their claims. This answer is usually followed by the following questions such as:

- "Well if that's the case, why do governments around the globe keep their existence a secret from the rest of mankind, who make up 99.9 percent of the populace living on the planet?"

- "Surely, wouldn't their advanced technology and Intelligence, by virtue of having mastered the secrets of Interstellar space travel, benefit all mankind and possible save the earth from certain destruction if we continue on our current path?"

- "Why would our so called elected or non-elected leaders not want to share those discoveries with its citizens?"

I usually look at those that ask these normal questions for a few moments, expecting the penny to drop at any moment, but sadly, it rarely does. They simply *cannot* comprehend such secrets can be deliberately withheld from the general public, or as is usually the case, ridiculed and debunked at every opportunity and for such a long time.

At this point, I get them to think about what else would change apart from the obvious benefits to our health, educational and technological advancements?

Slowly, they begin to touch on what I call the Big Three Distractions to a utopian society, where all men are truly equal, a world without pollution, poverty or hate, a world in harmony and at peace with itself. Nobel attributes one could associate or expect with an advanced civilization.

Money – The introduction of an advanced civilization's philosophy regarding the use of money, or lack of it, will be acceptable to a majority of the people on this planet. If the Visitors attitude to money is "we do not have money in our society" and they show us how they live and thrive, without any financial considerations, this will appeal to almost everyone but certainly not to the 3% who literally own all the resources that keep our financial systems in play. This leads naturally to the next big distraction…

Power – Without money, there is no power base to maintain. Without power you have no control over those you would like to see controlled. If you can't control the people, you become power-*less*. This of course throws up another problem in that if you become powerless, or are simply *perceived* to be powerless, you risk others who do *not* subscribe to the same 'no money policy' to gain power over you, dominate you and even exterminate you, if they have the means and will to do so. This naturally cannot be done in a global society that is totally fragmented in its beliefs and ideologies on how to effectively govern its own citizens.

Can you imagine a five star Army General being told he will no longer be getting his slice of a $600 Billion Dollar Defence budget to help protect his country because aliens landed at the white house and have shown us how to live without money? Can you equally imagine the heads of the world's top 50 *Global 500* companies subsequently losing ALL their money and collective power virtually overnight as stock markets go into free fall in response to a global demand for the creation of a hypothetical new U.N. ET/Earth Joint Co-Operation Initiative, to help move humanity into a new golden age? Can you imagine Royal Households and dictators all over the world drunk with power for centuries giving up their lineage and power just because we have established contact with ETs thousands if not Millions of years in advance of us? Can you imagine pharmaceutical, energy, legal, agricultural, aeronautical, educational, retail, mining and Industrial institutions all over the world, all of a sudden being made surplus to requirements, while we marvel and drool over the new technologies brought to us by the Visitors?

Religion - A by-product of power in some ways is religion as practiced today. The Visitors arrival and introduction to our society was probably best demonstrated in the late Carl Sagan's 1997 movie, CONTACT. The aliens arrival probably won't go down well with established religious orders and may even create new ones, based on misguided groups who may see the

Visitors as new age messiahs, setting the stage for even more religious confrontations, that may have unforeseen repercussions in the future. Apart from the real fear and possibility of the gradual break down of Buddhist, Hindu, Christian and Islamic organisations, many of the followers of these religions, will probably struggle with the new information these Visitors will bring and how best to reconcile their arrival, with existing doctrine and dogma. If these differences cannot be resolved it *could* lead to conflict.

As you can see, the reasons for the Visitors not coming out in full force and making their presence known to the entire world, (some would argue they already have) are indeed numerous and certainly not something our governments can afford to ignore, which I'm sure, they are well aware of.

Yet, can we afford to continue to pretend there are absolutely no alien vehicles invading our skies? Can we continue to prop up the possible illusion there are no extraterrestrial humanoids walking amongst us? Can we afford to ignore the avalanche of evidence in support of years of sworn eyewitness testimony and thousands upon thousands of first-hand accounts from credible eye witnesses, over the years?

What do we make of the data Joe brings up, regarding our vulnerability in this vast cosmos and the far future threat we face from any manner of natural cosmic 'accidents' such as the inevitable nearby supernova threat of Sirius B or rogue meteors, destined to hit us without warning? Was mankind designed to live and die on this earth, or do we have a greater destiny ahead? One that may involve us finally getting our act together, commence our own colonization projects, reach out to other civilizations beyond our solar system *as equals,* while exploring the secrets of the Universe in a peaceful, ethical and responsible manner.

Or do we simply stay put, continue to cut funding for Space Programs and research into new alternative energy sources and continue down the path of cover ups, lies, enslavement, war, poverty, discrimination, disinformation, abuse, pollution and the extinction of mankind on a dying planet? [At the time of finishing this book I was privileged to see Christopher Nolan's sci-fi master piece *Interstellar.* I find it rather fitting Nolan's primary message from the film mirrors exactly many of the points raised in this book.]*

The choice is ours and ours alone to make. I do not think anyone will come and save us. We simply have to *change* and prove we can change in order to continue our evolution as we usher in a new age of peace, harmony and exploration. Perhaps this is what *The Visitors* have been waiting for all along, for the children of Earth to grow up and join other sentient beings beyond the stars.

***

ADDENDUM

UFO's and the Extraterrestrial Enigma - OFFICIAL STATEMENTS

Here are a few well known and confirmed quotes on the matter, by various individuals since the 1940's right up to 2013. These quotes come from former Presidents, award winning scientists, Military Personnel, Government Officials, Pilots, Civilians, politicians, writers, Ph.D holders, and even religious leaders, all adding weight to the growing body of evidence that we may not be alone and that Earth may have been visited by beings from other worlds far more advanced than ours.

"In my mind, there is no question that they're out there. My Career is well established. My texts books are required reading in all the major capitals on planet earth. If you want to become a physicist to learn about the unified field theory-you read my books. Therefore, I'm in a position to say: Yes- Most likely they're out there, perhaps even visited, perhaps on our moon." - ABC News Quote

Professor Michio Kaku Author of Theoretical Physics UNY

"I've been convinced for a long time that the flying saucers are real and interplanetary. In other words we are being watched by beings from outer space."
Albert M. Chop, deputy public relations director, National Aeronautics and Space Administration,(NASA) and former United States Air Force spokesman for Project Blue Book.

"When the long awaited solution to the UFO problem comes, I believe that it will prove to be not merely the next small step in the march of science, but a mighty and totally unexpected quantum leap." "We had a job to do, whether right or wrong, to keep the public from getting excited"
Dr J Allen Hynek, Director US Air Force´s project Blue Book as a scientific consultant, astronomer, investigator and analysis.

"Of course it is possible that UFOs really do contain aliens as many people believe, and the Government is hushing it up."
Professor Stephen Hawking

"Given the millions of billions of Earth-like planets, life elsewhere in the Universe without a doubt, does exist. In the vastness of the Universe we are not alone."
The Bible According to Albert Einstein

"It is my thesis that flying saucers are real and that they are space ships from another solar system. There is no doubt in my mind that these objects are interplanetary craft of some sort. I and my colleagues are confident that they do not originate in our solar system."
Dr Herman Oberth (The father of modern rocketry)

"I am completely convinced that UFOs have an out-of-world basis."
Dr Walther Riedel (Once chief designer and research director at the German rocket center in Peenemunde)

"The least improbable explanation is that these things are artificial and controlled ... My opinion for some time has been that they have an extraterrestrial origin."
Dr Maurice Biot (leading aerodynamicists and mathematical physicist)

"The evidence is overwhelming that Planet Earth is being visited by intelligently controlled extraterrestrial spacecraft. In other words, SOME UFOs are alien spacecraft. Most are not. It's clear from the Opinion Polls and my own experience, that indeed most people accept the notion that SOME UFOs are alien spacecraft. The greater the education, the MORE likely to accept this proposition"
Stanton Friedman Defence Contractor Nuclear Physicist

"Extraterrestrial contact is a real phenomenon. The Vatican is receiving much information about extraterrestrials and their contacts with humans from its Nuncios (embassies) in various countries, such as Mexico, Chile and Venezuela."
Monsignor Corrado Balducci As stated 5 different times on Italian TV** (Vatican theologian insider close to the Pope, Monsignor Balducci said that he is on a Vatican commission looking into extraterrestrial encounters, and how to cope with the emerging general realization of extraterrestrial contact.)

"We must insist upon full access to disks recovered. For instance, in the LA case the Army grabbed it and would not let us have it for cursory examination."
J Edgar Hoover

"I am convinced that these objects do exist and that they are not manufactured by any nations on earth"
Air Chief Marshal Lord Dowding (Commander-in-chief, Royal Air Force Fighter Command)

"The UFO phenomenon being reported is something real and not visionary or fictitious"
General Nathan Twining Chairman, Joint chiefs of staff, 1955-1958

"With control of the universe at stake, a crash program is imperative. We produced the A-bomb, under the huge Manhattan Project, in an amazingly short time. The needs, the urgency today are even greater. The Air Force should end UFO secrecy, give the facts to scientists, the public, to Congress. Once the people realize the truth, they would back, even demand a crash program...for this is one race we dare not lose."
Major Donald E Keyhoe USMC, Director NICAP 1953

"...the next war will be an interplanetary war. The nations of the earth must someday make a common front against attack by people from other planets. The politics of the future will be cosmic or interplanetary" (1955)
Gen. Douglas MacArthur

"I can assure you that flying saucers, given that they exist, are not constructed by any power on earth"
President Harry S. Truman

"I think about how quickly our differences worldwide would vanish if we were facing an alien threat from outside this world. And I ask you, does not this threat already exist?"
President Ronald Reagan - A United Nations formal address.

"The phenomenon of UFOs does exist, and it must be treated seriously."
Mikhail Gorbachev

"I'm not at liberty to discuss the government's knowledge of extraterrestrial UFOs at this time. I am still personally being briefed on the subject!"
President Richard M. Nixon

"Condemnation without investigation is the height of ignorance."
Albert Einstein[56]

"Mission control, we have a UFO pacing our position, request instructions!"
Astronaut Cady Coleman NASA transmission shuttle mission STS-73

"I've been asked about UFOs and I've said publicly I thought they were somebody else, some other civilization."
Commander Eugene Cernan, Commanded the Apollo 17 Mission. (LA TIMES, 1973)

"We have contact with alien cultures."
Astronaut Dr Brian O'Leary

"In my official status, I cannot comment on ET contact. However, personally, I can assure you, we are not alone!
Charles J. Camarda (Ph.D.) NASA Astronaut

"UFO sightings are now so common, the military doesn't have time to worry about them - so they screen them out. The major defence systems have UFO filters built into them, and when a UFO appears, they simply ignore it."
Lee Katchen (former atmospheric physicist with NASA)

"All Apollo and Gemini flights were followed, both at a distance and sometimes also quite closely, by space vehicles of extraterrestrial origin - flying saucers, or UFOs, if you want to call them by that name. Every time it occurred, the astronauts informed Mission Control, who then ordered absolute silence."
Maurice Chatelain, former chief of NASA Communications Systems.

"At no time, when the astronauts were in space were they alone: there was a constant surveillance by UFOs."
NASA's Scott Carpenter

On May 11, 1962 NASA pilot Joseph Walker said that one of his tasks was to detect UFOs during his X-15 flights. He had filmed five or six UFOs during his record breaking fifty-mile-high flight in April, 1962. It was the second time he had filmed UFOs in flight. To date none of those films has been released to the public for viewing. During a lecture at the Second National Conference on the Peaceful Uses of Space Research in Seattle, Washington, he stated:
"I don't feel like speculating about them. All I know is what appeared on the film which was developed after the flight."
NASA Pilot Joseph A. Walker

"The evidence points to the fact that Roswell was a real incident and that indeed an alien craft did crash, and that material was recovered from that site. We all know that UFOs are real. All we need to ask is where they come from, and what do they want?"
Capt. Edgar Mitchell Apollo 14 Astronaut

"I was testing a P-51 fighter in Minneapolis when I spotted this object. I was at about 10,000 feet on a nice, bright, sunny afternoon. I thought the object was a kite, then I realized that no kite is gonna fly that high. As I got closer it looked like a weather balloon, gray and about three feet in diameter. But as soon as I got behind the darn thing it didn't look like a balloon anymore. It looked like a saucer, a disk. About the same time, I realized that it was suddenly going away from me -- and there I was, running at about 300 miles per hour. I tracked it for a little way, and then all of a sudden the damn thing just took off. It pulled about a 45 degree climbing turn and accelerated and just flat disappeared."
Mercury Astronaut Capt. Donald Slayton

"Something is going on in the skies that we do not understand. If all the airline pilots and Air Force pilots who have seen UFOs – and sometimes chased them – have been the victims of hallucinations, then an awful lot of pilots should be taken off and forbidden to fly."
Captain Kervendal

"At no time, when the astronauts were in space were they alone: there was a constant surveillance by UFOs."
Astronaut Scott Carpenter

"This was no ordinary UFO. Scores of people saw it. It was no illusion, no deception, and no imagination."
Air Marshall Azim Daudpota

"From their manoeuvres and their terrific speed I am certain their flight performance was greater than any aircraft known today."
Colonel Carl Sanderson

"The matter is the most highly classified subject in the United States Government, rating even higher than the H Bomb. Flying saucers exist. Their Modus operandi is unknown but concentrated effort is being made by a small group headed by Doctor Vannevar Bush."
Wilbert Smith

"Look, I have a pension to worry about. I have a family to take care of, and they told me to just back away from this entirely or else."
Astronaut James Irwin

"UFOs are impossible to deny. It is very strange that we have never been able to find out the source for over two decades."
Colonel Fuijo Hayashi

"Many of the reports that cannot be explained have come from intelligent and technically well-qualified individuals whose integrity cannot be doubted."
Major General E.B. LeBaily

"For thirty years, I've held that image in my mind. What I saw was a circular object that looked like two pie plates put on top of each other with a golf ball on top. It was a classic flying sauce, and it shot a beam of something at our warhead"
Lieutenant Robert M. Jacobs

"I am completely convinced that [UFOs] have an out-of-world basis."
Dr Walther Riedel

"UFOs sighted in Indonesia are identical with those sighted in other countries. Sometimes they pose a problem for our Air Defence and once we were obliged to open fire on them."
Air Marshall Nurjadin Roesmin

"Maximum security exists concerning the subject of UFOs."
Allen Dulles

EXTRATERRESTRIAL HUMANOID REPORTS AROUND THE WORLD

C urtsey of Alberto Rosales and his incredible work in documenting alien humanoid contacts around the world, I have selected a hand full of cases featuring *human looking aliens* from literally hundreds of cases in Alberto's vast database.

Minas Gerais, Brazil (exact location not given)

Date: November 15 1990

Time: night

*A man and his vehicle were taking inside a hovering disc shaped craft. Inside he was met by **tall human like beings** that identified themselves as visitors from **Alpha Centauri**. There was much communication. No other information.*

***

Location.Teba Malaga Spain

Date: September 14 1975

Time: Midnight

Two young girls were standing and chatting by their front door when both saw a tiny shiny object descend slowly towards them, one of the girls thinking it was a piece of aluminium foil walked back into the house. The

289

other girl remained, looking at the object realizing it was something more mysterious.

She was last seen bending down apparently in an effort to pick up the tiny object. Almost an hour later she still had not entered the house. He parents and friends now alarmed realized she was missing and alerted the local Civil Guard Unit. A fruitless searched ensued. The next night the young girl was seen walking into town with **two tall blond strangers***, a woman and a man.*

They walked the young girl to her house, always holding her by the hand and dropped her off, telling her before leaving that they would one day see her again. The girl could not recall a single detail of where she had been for the last 24 hours, her memory was totally blank. The last thing she remembered was bending down to pick up the tiny shiny object.

***

Location. New Orleans Louisiana

Date: November 11, 1975

Time: Night

The witness was sitting outside when she saw a large disc over the house. Suddenly she found herself apparently inside the object. There she confronted by several tall, **human-like humanoids with long blond hair** *that communicated with her via telepathy. She was shown around and later returned back to her house. Later that night together with her husband, watched two disks flying over their house. A large circle of flattened grass was found near the house the next day, which turned brown and remained that colour for a few years.*

***

Remote Viewing UFOS and The Visitors

Location, Ris, near Oslo Norway

Date: Late Summer 1974

Time: Evening

*A woman was working in a field when she spotted a metallic oval shaped craft descending close to her. She could hear what sounded like some unknown type of music emanating from the object as it landed only 3 meters from the witness. As the craft landed a door opened and **three 2 meter tall men with long blond hair** and wearing dark **tight-fitting blue flight suits** emerged. Using friendly gestures, the strangers invite the witness on board the craft. Afraid, she refuses and runs away from the area. She never saw the strangers or the object depart. It took several years before the witness was able to speak about her experience. The witness had a good reputation in her town.*

***

Location. Between Jerez de la Frontera & Trebujena, Cadiz Spain

Date July, 1974

Time- 23:30

A young man and his girlfriend watched a silent round orange light passing slowly low over the area. It crossed the main highway then landed on top of a nearby hill. Climbing to the top, there he encounters two other men that had seen a circular object with a transparent cupola on top, with two moving shadows inside. The main witness now saw the object ascend and fly towards another nearby hill. He follows the object with his motor cycle but loses sight of it. He then becomes confused and notices a strange silence in the area. He then sees a large moving truck and follows it, after rounding a curve he realises that the truck had disappeared into thin air. He turns on his high beams and sees a bright orange object with a crystal like cupola on the ground by the side of the road.

The witness signals the object several times with his lights but gets no response. He then drives towards the lighted object but it suddenly vanishes, in its place he sees two large silent automobiles approaching slowly, he approaches the vehicles and sees two men and a woman in the first car and a man in the second.

*They are all described as **tall, blond and Nordic in appearance**. They asked the witness several questions then drove off. The witness suffered a nervous breakdown soon after the incident and also felt the strange Nordic looking people in the vehicles were somehow connected with the UFOS*

Source: Balleser Olmos & fernandex Peri, Enciclopedia De Los Encuentros cercanos con Ovnis

***

Location. Over South Vietnam (Exact location not provided)

Date: 1966

Time: Night

The crew of a B-52 during a night-time mission over South Vietnam, encountered a craft that measured approximately ¼ mile in diameter and was estimated by the crew to be 700 feet high, with 23 levels located in the upper dome, the crew made reference to seeing "windows" on each "floor", and identified the outline of possible beings or humanoids. The craft departed at an extremely high rate of speed and opened up a local space/time "hole/Window" exposing blue sky and clouds.

***

Location. West Bromwich England

Date: late November 1975   Time: 00:05 a.m.

His father awaked the witness and from the front bedroom window they both watched an upside down saucer shaped craft with a dome on top drift slowly above the rooftops. It was completely silent. It had rotating multi-coloured lights around its flattened base. The craft also had two or three rectangular shaped windows inset into the dome. The windows were brightly lit and two standing figures could be seen inside. These appeared to be man like and had **long blond or golden hair**. The object finally disappeared from sight behind some nearby houses.

HC addition # 1500

Source: Steve Gerrard, quoting Northern UFO News # 150

***

Location. Siracusa, Sicily Italy

Date: October 1973   Time: 09:00 a.m.

The witness was alone in her house taking a bath, when suddenly an intense bright light appeared on the wall of the bathroom. At the center of the light, a human like shape began to take form. It became a very tall man with **light blond shoulder length hair, pale features, and large beautiful eyes**. The witness could not speak but was frightened, the man smiled then vanished. The witness felt a mental message telling her to go outside. She ran to the balcony in time to see a huge disc shaped object passing slowly over the house.

HC addition # 558

Source: Angel Franchetto, Los Extraterrestres

Y Nuestro Futuro

***

Location. Lerida Catalonia Spain

Date: August 1979   Time: night

The witness along with a friend was staying in her second floor apartment when she began to feel an oppressive atmosphere around her, especially in her head, wrist, and ankles. She suddenly floated out the open window and then vaguely recalls being in a huge dome full of crying people. Two men that took her into a gray metallic clinical looking room suddenly seized her.

She was left lying on a bed. Next to her stood two very tall beings wearing white robes, they had shoulder length gold colored hair, but she could not recall any facial features, another tall being appeared and took her by the hand. **This being had a serene beautiful human face full of wisdom and compassion.** She later awoke in her bed after she had felt a sting like a pinprick.

HC addition # 210

Source: Antonio Ribera, Intl. UFO Magazine

Vol. # 2

***

Remote Viewing UFOS and The Visitors

Location. Playa De Salgueiros, Douro Litoral, Portugal

Date: September 25 1983   Time: 01:30 a.m.

J. F. M., 25, an agronomist and his girlfriend, M. F. B. R., 26, were camping in a wooded area at about ½ km from the beach, something they did every weekend. Suddenly their attention was drawn to a strange low frequency sound, like a 'motor'. After about 20 minutes, as his girlfriend slept, the man stepped out of the tent and noticed a very bright spinning light towards the southwest at about 1,000 meters away.

It appeared to be over a field that surrounded the beach area, at the same level of the tent. The light, which was orange in colour, illuminated a large area of the field, like that of a maritime beacon, with a cadence of three seconds interval.

Moments later the witness noticed two more objects, one on each side of the light, very close to each the light and clearly illuminated by it. These two objects were apparently resting on the ground on three 'pillar-like' protrusions. The objects were about 5 or 6 meters in diameter. Soon he detected the presence of four humanoid figures standing next to the objects.

They were completely human in appearance, of normal stature (1.70 and 1.80 m) and very similar to each other, giving the appearance of being masculine in nature except for one figure that was more feminine in appearance. *They were all wearing a white coverall like outfit, which covered their bodies completely. The bright light illuminated the figures clearly, in a rapid blinking manner.*

The figures at first were bunched up together, but some began to walk slowly almost like "in slow motion". The figures moved away in different directions, moving at about 5 meters away from the object. However after a few minutes they returned to the vicinity of the objects. They gave the

295

impression of having reconnoitre the terrain in a symmetrical form or manner, all inclined towards the ground.

While the bright light maintained its cadence and illuminated the area the figures remained visible, as this happened, the two other objects suddenly lifted up simultaneously and flew very quickly towards the southwest in an oblique trajectory, the objects then returned to their original location. Meanwhile the humanoids suddenly disappeared from sight. 20 minutes had gone by. Suddenly all three UFOs then slowly flew over the terrain and then returned to their original position and then again left this time in an ascending oblique trajectory and very fast on a northwest direction.

At that same moment some red lights appeared on the top of the objects; these quickly disappeared in the sky in a matter of seconds. 10 minutes later the girlfriend already awake, they heard noises outside and when they looked out they spotted the three UFOs in the same location. These then rose up and flew at about 10meters from the ground along the coast in a northerly direction. They seemed to be darker this time and after performing some manoeuvres, disappeared from sight, this time for good.

HC addition # 111

Source: *Vicente-Juan Ballester Olmos, & Juan A. Fernandez Peri*

Enciclopedia de Los Encuentros cercanos con OVNIS
Type: C

Translated by Albert S Rosales

***

Another Peruvian Contactee

Location. Callao, Peru

Remote Viewing UFOS and The Visitors

Date: February 28 1972   *Time: unknown*

35-year old Carlos Belevan Mesinas reportedly came in contact with **human-looking aliens** *from the* **Sirius star system***. The alien's skin was tanned (like African American, but not entirely black) dark brown in colour. They were of medium height (about 1.8 m) dressed in tight fitting overalls, with helmets, black belts and big black high boots.*

Their eyes were light green and transparent. Their hair was light chestnut in colour. There were 4 aliens, and they told him their names and positions in the crew. Their leader was called "Arut". The aliens told Mesinas that they lived in 4 planets around the Hipparcos 30344 star system in the Canis Maggioris constellation. The witness experienced additional contacts until June 1974.

The aliens reportedly have a colony of 256 humans in their planet. They build their homes out of volcanic materials and polymers. Water in their planet is fresh, they lack salt water. They purportedly used bases on the moon whenever they visit the earth.

Corrected update: *The aliens told Mesinas that they originated from an area near Sirius; the exact location was later established to be the orange star HD52698 in Canis Maggioris constellation, 47 light years away. Aliens gave the names of their planets as, Nex-Aar, Niks, Nuks and Ner. Their star system is called Karks. The main planet was Nex-Aar, its capital Kab-Ver (population 23 million). The aliens had lunar bases in several Solar systems as well as bases in one of the satellites of Jupiter.*

HC addendum

Source: Anton Anfalov

***

Location. Bissoe Truro Cornwall England

Date: January 29 1979   Time: 02:00 a.m.

*A man and his son were suddenly awakened to find their bedroom brightly lit up. One of the witnesses looked out the window and was amazed to see a bright hovering oval shaped craft. Inside two human like figures with **long fair wavy hair** could be clearly seen. The bright object then glided silently away and shot away at high speed.*

HC addition # 1435

Source: Bob Boyd, Plymouth UFO Research Group
Type: A

***

Location. Takamatsu, Kagawa-ken Hokkaido Japan

Date: September 1 1984   Time: 1800

A six-year old girl named Nao Nishimoto was playing with her friends riding bicycles in the front yard of her apartment. Young Nao went to the end of the yard on her bike when she saw a large round luminous object in the sky over the rice field. She stopped at the fence and stared intently at the object, but she didn't call to her friends. The brilliant object was coming in from the right, and as it became closer and bigger, she perceived a large ring of colourful lights flying outside the object at the same time.

To her surprise, the ring was just like a huge necklace with brilliant beads of many kinds of colours. As it approached the front yard its shape changed from a cross to a rectangle, then to a circle. It was a very beautiful sight and as the hazy outlines of the luminous craft became clear, the "necklace" disappeared. The object appeared to be shape like a large bell as it first came in a zigzag movement over the rice field. When it hovered a

298

few meters from the field for a while, the ears of the rice plants swayed as if in a wind.

Then the domed saucer moved to the left and hovered near a kindergarten school. It was only about 25 meters distant from the girl, so she could see its cabin as large as six or eight mat rooms of a Japanese house. According to Nao, the UFO had a large dome with four portholes and a small golden ball on the top, which was very bright. Three large circular structures protruded at the bottom.

The colour of the hull gradually changed from orange into silver. While Nao stared at the fantastic ship, a nice looking little boy appeared at one of the four round windows---the second one from the left---and when he looked at the girl standing at the fence, the boy smiled showing his white teeth to her great surprise.

Nao said the boy she saw had long hair, pulled back from his face and it reached his shoulders. **His hair was golden in colour and his face was round**. Nao said his skin colour was the same as hers; he had large round eyes, small nose and ears.

Nao said she only saw the upper half of the boy. So it seemed that his shirt was grey and a little shiny. His shirt had a V-shaped neckline. She felt sure he was a boy because of his eyes. As Nao watched, the craft flew over the roof of the kindergarten and disappeared. Nao followed a path that led to the tableland or mesa of nearby Mt. Yashima and again saw the craft now hovering low over some fields. She saw the "boy" at the window, which immediately smiled again and waved his left hand.

At first he slowly raised his hand showing the palm, then he let it down, and again he raised the hand slowly. The sleeves of his clothing were long enough to reach the wrists. Soon after that the craft began to circle over the rice field in addition to rotating on its axis and flew toward the mountain.

When it came to the top of the mountain, about 300 meters above the sea, the ship flashed twice and suddenly disappeared.

HC addition # 790

Source: Hachiro Kubota, FSR Vol. 31 # 1
Type: A

High Strangeness Index: 7

Reliability of Source: 7

****

UFO Staffordshire, UK - October 1954

Jessie Roestenberg and her Children

In October, 1954, in Staffordshire, UK, Jessie Roestenberg was in her small cottage, while her two sons were outside.

Mrs. Roestenberg then heard a very strange sound. According to her it sounded like water being poured on a fire. Her first thoughts were of her children, afraid that a plane might have crashed landed. She then proceeded to go outside to investigate further only to find her two sons lying flat out on the ground in front of the house.

The two boys cried out, "Mommy, Mommy there's a flying saucer". At first Jessie did not believe them till she looked up and saw what she could only describe a huge Mexican hat type object, with a silver shinny metallic look. It was indeed a flying saucer. It stood stationary in mid-air above the barn house in the distance.

*The object had a dome on top, through which she could see two occupants. She described them as **'beautiful' with long golden hair**. The occupants wore a **pale-blue ski-type jumper suit**. [Note the similarity with the beings described by Travis Walton in 1975]The craft was tilted toward Jessie and her sons so she could clearly see the two occupants, the hair resembled the old kings page boy type cut, curled up at the shoulders.*

Already gripped with fear she looked at her sons and asked if they both could see what she was seeing which they acknowledged and by the time she looked back. The craft was gone. She asked her sons where the object was and they both pointed up to a small dot in the sky.

Then as if to say a final farewell, the UFO came down, circled the large barn three times in the air, and then shot away into the sky.

Terrified, Jessie grabbed the boys and ran straight back into the house where they hid under the kitchen table till her husband came back from work. The story made the local and National news briefly and Jessie suffered ridicule but to her credit has never changed her story. Her sons refuse to comment on what they saw that fateful day.

Jessie Roestenberg – Photo from Google Images (source unknown)

You can watch a video of Jessie on YouTube describing her amazing encounter as witnessed by her two sons.
https://www.youtube.com/watch?v=x979IEyjoy8

These are just a handful of reports I have selected at random, but there are literally thousands of similar cases reported all over the world. A majority of these cases can once again be found at *The Humanoid Sighting Reports & Journal of Humanoid Studies* [57]website

Alberto Rosales's incredible online database has thousands of records extending as far back as 4780BC. I wholeheartedly recommend serious investigators and the open minded reader to take some time to explore and investigate these cases for your selves and reach your *own* conclusions in the absence of any government announcement or support, backing up the reality of extraterrestrial visitation to our planet.

EPILOGUE:

The Travis Walton Case:
The forgotten witness?

While in the middle of writing this book, I received some correspondence from a friend of mine, Lawrence Digges, who happened to also be a moderator in TKR, one of Remote Viewing's largest online projects. I had informed a few close RV colleagues about the Walton case which generated a great deal of interest with emails going back and forth. Lawrence revealed he had some rather remarkable information directly related to this case. I'll let you read his story which adds support to the logger's claims of a UFO seen on that fateful night.

Date: 28 Sep 2012 05:51

*So as you know, I'm from Phoenix, Arizona originally. The story goes, my grandparents were camping in the White Mountains in the Heber area. It was deer hunting season and my Grandfather was an avid hunter. Grandpa had already gone to sleep but my Grandmother was still awake, doing things outside the tent. Suddenly, she saw this incredible "red light" silently and slowly move over the mountain. She watched it for some time until it moved on without a sound. **She knew she had seen something incredible** - she just didn't know what.*

Remote Viewing UFOS and The Visitors

When they got back to Phoenix after their few days in the mountains, Grandma told my mom about what she had seen. By that time, it was all over the news in Phoenix that a man from Snowflake, AZ had disappeared right in that area on that same night etc... Grandma hadn't heard the news about it yet but mom had and they put two and two together.

You have to understand; my grandmother was a very no-nonsense woman of old school values and ways. Although she did have a noted knack for psi, she was certainly not prone to wild stories of any kind, flights of fancy or practical jokes.

By the time my mom told me all this one day, when it casually came up in conversation, my grandmother had had a stroke and I couldn't ask her about it to hear the story first hand. I did ask my grandfather about it however, and he confirmed that they were camping in that area when "that boy" disappeared. And that yes, Grandma "thought she saw something," although he added he thinks it was probably just a helicopter (...)

So as it stands, my grandmother saw the UFO that abducted Travis Walton.

-L

Bibliography
(Remote Viewing, UFOS and ESP)

- MIND TREK Exploring Consciousness, Time and Space through Remote Viewing, Joseph McMoneagle Hampton Roads Publishing Company
- THE ULTIMATE TIME MACHINE Joseph McMoneagle, Hampton Roads Publishing Company.
- REMOTE VIEWING SECRETS Joseph McMoneagle, Hampton Roads Publishing Company.
- EVERYBODY'S GUIDE TO NATURAL ESP, Ingo Swann
- PENETRATION: The Question of Extraterrestrial and Human Telepathy, Ingo Swann Books, 1998
- READING THE ENEMY'S MIND inside Star Gate – America's Psychic Espionage Program - Maj Paul H. Smith Ph.D (USA ret)
- THE REALITY OF ESP – A physicist's proof of psychic abilities Russell Targ - Quest Books
- ESP WARS EAST & WEST – May, Rubel, Auerbach LFR 2014
- THE SEVENTH SENSE – Lyn Buchannan
- REMOTE VIEWING – David Morehouse
- VOICES FROM THE COSMOS – C.B. Scott Jones PhD and Angela T Smith PhD
- DIARY OF AN ABDUCTION - Angela T Smith PhD
- ANAMOLOUS COGNITION – May/Marwaha
- CRV CONTROLLED REMOTE VIEWING – Daz Smith
- THE INDEFINITE BOUNDARY – Guy Lyon Playfair
- MIND TO MIND – Warcollier

Remote Viewing UFOS and The Visitors

- REMOTE VIEWING: The Science and Theory of Nonphysical Perception, Courtney Brown PhD
- OPENING TO THE INFINITE Stephan A Schwartz
- BEYOND REINCARNATION – Joe H. Slate PhD
- ALTERED STATES OF CONSCIOUSNESS Charles T. Tart
- UFO DYNAMICS: Psychiatric and Psychic Aspects of the UFO Syndrome, Eric Schwarz Berthold
- GEORGE ADMASKI The untold Story Lou Zinsstag & Timothy Good
- REMOTE VIEWERS: The Secret History of America's Psychic Spies, Jim Schnabel, Jan 1997
- WONDERS IN THE SKY – Jacques Vallee and Chris Aubeck
- EARTH AN ALIEN ENTERPRISE – Timothy Good
- EXTRATERRESTRIAL ARCHAEOLOGY – David Hatcher Childress
- UFOS ARE WITH US - TAKE MY WORD – Leo Dworshak
- MAJIC EYES ONLY – Ryan S. Wood
- PALE SKIN, GIANTS AND THE GREAT TRANSITION – Milton E. Brener
- THE GREAT APPARITIONS OF MARY – Ingo Swann

RV Websites and Links

http://www.dojopsi.com Palyne PJ Gaenir

http://www.remoteviewed.com/ Daz Smith

http://www.mceagle.com Joseph W McMoneagle

https://www.monroeinstitute.org/ The Monroe institute

http://lfr.org (LFR, home of) Cognitive Sciences Laboratory

http://www.farsight.org Courtney Brown PhD

http://www.biomindsuperpowers.com/ Ingo Swann

http://www.mprv.net/one20.html Jon Knowles

http://rviewer.com/ Paul H. Smith PhD

http://www.crviewer.com/ Lyn Buchanan

http://mindwiseconsulting.com/ Angela Thompson Smith PhD

https://davidmorehouse.com/ David Morehouse PhD

A full and comprehensive list of Remote Viewing resources and sites can be found at the International Remote Viewing Associations (IRVA) official website http://www.irva.org/resources/links.html

INDEX

311

About the Author

Tunde Atunrase is an IT Analyst Supervisor by profession. He was first introduced to RV back in 1995, and was formally trained in 2001. He has taken part in numerous private and public demonstrations of Remote Viewing, often volunteering his skills towards projects such as the recent award winning 2014 IRVA Warcollier Prize. Tunde loves reading, writing poetry, watching movies, playing keyboards and travelling. He has two daughters, currently lives in London and is working on his next project. For further information or contact details, the author can be reached at tundeatunrase24@gmail.com

NOTES

---

[1] Jim Schnable REMOTE VIEWERS: The Secret History of America's Psychic Spies, Jim Schnabel, Jan 1997

[2] Remote Viewers: The Secret History of America's Psychic Spies – Jim Schnabel.

[3] The complete RV protocol TKR Paylyn 'PJ' Ganier http://www.dojopsi.info/tenthousandroads/rvprotocol.shtml

[4] Joseph McMoneagle MIND TREK Exploring Consciousness, Time and Space through REMOTE VIEWING, Hampton Roads Publishing Company.

[5] Russell Targ THE REALITY OF ESP – A physicist's proof of psychic abilities – chapter 6 Taking ESP to the Army.

[6] A full description of this session including session sketches can be found in issue 10 of Eightmartinis http://www.eightmartinis.com/eight-martinis-issue-10

[7] Prudence Calabrese - International UFO Conference 8th Annual Convention lecture 1999 DVD

[8] Joe McMoneagle, MIND TREK Exploring Consciousness, Time, and Space Through REMOTE VIEWING, Page 243

[9] http://en.wikipedia.org/wiki/Ingo_Swann Swann's Jupiter Rings

[10] Heavenly Lights, The Apparitions of Fatima and the UFO Phenomenon, Dr Joaquim Fernandez/Fina D'Armada, pages 107.

[11] http://en.wikipedia.org/wiki/L%C3%BAcia_Santos

[12] Heavenly Lights, The Apparitions of Fatima and the UFO Phenomenon, Dr Joaquim Fernandes/Fina D'Armada, page 11, The day of May 13th

[13] Heavenly Lights, The Apparitions of Fatima and the UFO Phenomenon, Dr Joaquim Fernandes/Fina D'Armada, Page 179 chapter Thermal Effects.

[14] Heavenly Lights, The Apparitions of Fatima and the UFO Phenomenon, Dr Joaquim Fernandes/Fina D'Armada, Page 179 chapter Thermal Effects.

[15] Heavenly Lights, The Apparitions of Fatima and the UFO Phenomenon, Dr Joaquim Fernandes/Fina D'Armada, Page 179 chapter Thermal Effects.

[16] Heavenly Lights, The Apparitions of Fatima and the UFO Phenomenon, Dr Joaquim Fernandes/Fina D'Armada, Pages 166-167.

[17] http://www.wired.com/thisdayintech/2009/09/0925vitim-meteorite/

[18] Transcript taken from A Ray Of Light On Fatima published in 1974 by Filipe Furtado de Mendonca

[19] Celestial Secrets, The Hidden History of The Fatima Cover Up, Dr Joaquim Fernandes/Fina D'Armada, page 14, Chapter - Fatima Apparitions Predicted.

[20] Celestial Secrets, The Hidden History of The Fatima Cover Up, Dr Joaquim Fernandes/Fina D'Armada, page 14, Chapter - Fatima Apparitions Predicted.

[21] Carlos Diaz Hoax Bill Hamilton http://www.rense.com/general6/hoax.htm

[22] Carlos Diaz Hoax http://www.rense.com/general6/hoax.htm

[23] http://www.richplanet.net/rp_genre.php?ref=124&part=1&gen=1

[24] http://www.richplanet.net/rp_genre.php?ref=124&part=1&gen=1

[25] http://www.louthleader.co.uk/news/local/ufo-investigator-backs-triangle-spacecraft-claims-1-1012412

[26] A tokamak is a device using a magnetic field to confine a plasma in the shape of a torus. Achieving a stable plasma equilibrium requires magnetic field lines that move around the torus in a helical shape. Such a helical field can be

generated by adding a toroidal field (traveling around the torus in circles) and a poloidal field (traveling in circles orthogonal to the toroidal field). In a tokamak, the toroidal field is produced by electromagnets that surround the torus, and the poloidal field is the result of a toroidal electric current that flows inside the plasma. This current is induced inside the plasma with a second set of electromagnets. The tokamak is one of several types of magnetic confinement devices, and is one of the most-researched candidates for producing controlled thermonuclear fusion power http://en.wikipedia.org/wiki/Tokamak

[27] http://en.wikipedia.org/wiki/2007_Alderney_UFO_sighting

[28] http://en.wikipedia.org/wiki/2007_Alderney_UFO_sighting

[29] http://en.wikipedia.org/wiki/2007_Alderney_UFO_sighting

[30] http://en.wikipedia.org/wiki/2007_Alderney_UFO_sighting

[31] Delta Shape Hybrid Patent http://www.google.co.uk/patents/US7093789

[32] Boeing Hybrid Airship Patent Report
http://www.google.co.uk/patents/US7093789

[33] US Patent Report http://www.google.co.uk/patents/US7093789

[34] Ben R Rich quote – Timothy Good, Earth and Alien Enterprise 2013

[35] John Borroughs on Lt. Col Malcolm Zickler
http://backtobentwaters.blogspot.co.uk/2009/07/open-letter-to-gen.html

[36] 244 Page document http://www.examiner.com/article/rendelsham-exposed-government-inside-job-no-ufo-time-traveling-aliens-present

[37] Sascha Christie – Rendlesham Hoax
http://www.examiner.com/article/rendelsham-exposed-government-inside-job-no-ufo-time-traveling-aliens-present

[38] http://www.theufochronicles.com/2015/04/triangular-shaped-ufo-sighted-at-nellis.html

[39] Dr Ardy Sixkiller Clark – (Three Military Veterans Describe and Encounter) Encounters With Star people Anomalis Books 2012

[40] Nick Redfern – Close Encounters Of The Fatal Kind New Page Books 2014 – The Microwave Incident

[41] Nick Redfern – Close Encounters Of The Fatal Kind New Page Books 2014 – The Microwave Incident

[42] The crew http://en.wikipedia.org/wiki/Japan_Air_Lines_flight_1628_incident

[43] John Calllahan 1 http://en.wikipedia.org/wiki/Japan_Air_Lines_flight_1628_incident

[44] John Callahan 2 http://en.wikipedia.org/wiki/Japan_Air_Lines_flight_1628_incident#cite_note-Callahan-18

[45] John Callahan 3 http://en.wikipedia.org/wiki/Japan_Air_Lines_flight_1628_incident

[46] Ross 154 (1) http://en.wikipedia.org/wiki/Ross_154

[47] Ross 154 - http://www.solstation.com/stars/ross154.htm

[48] Travis Walton http://www.travis-walton.com/abduction.html

[49] Travis Walton Fire In the Sky http://www.travis-walton.com/aliens.html

[50] Wikipedia on Alpha Centauri Bb http://en.wikipedia.org/wiki/Alpha_Centauri_Bb

[51] Wikipedia on Alpha Centauri Bb Xavier Dumusque http://en.wikipedia.org/wiki/Alpha_Centauri_Bb

[52] Wikipedia on Alpha Centauri Bb – Detection http://en.wikipedia.org/wiki/Alpha_Centauri_Bb

[53] Wikipedia on Alpha Centauri Bb – Detection
http://en.wikipedia.org/wiki/Alpha_Centauri_Bb

[54] Wikipedia on Alpha Centauri B and The possibility of more planets being detected - http://en.wikipedia.org/wiki/Alpha_Centauri_Bb

[55] Ultimate Time Machine Joe McMoneagle

[56]

https://sites.google.com/site/paranormalzonex/UFOs/ufo_and_extraterrestrial_life Famous Quotes

[57] Humanoid Sighting Reports & Journal of Humanoid Studies -
http://www.ufoinfo.com/humanoid/index.shtml

Made in the USA
Columbia, SC
29 August 2017